LEADERSHIP REBORN:
8 WAYS FAITH TRANSFORMS YOUR EVERYDAY LEADERSHIP

Larry Ely and Daniel Ely

Copyright ©2025 by Larry Ely and Daniel Ely.
Leadership Reborn: 8 Ways Faith Transforms Your Everyday Leadership.
Published by Leadership Books, Inc. Las Vegas, NV – New York, NY
LeadershipBooks.com

ISBN: 9781965401279 (Hardcover)
9781965401286 (Paperback)
Category: Christian Living, Spiritual Growth, Leadership

All Rights Reserved. No part of this publication may be reproduced, distributed, or transmitted in any form or by any means, including photocopying, recording, or other electronic or mechanical methods without the prior written permission of the publisher, except in the case of brief quotations embodied in critical reviews and certain other noncommercial uses permitted by copyright law.

Leadership Books, Inc. is committed to publishing works of quality and integrity. In that spirit, we are proud to offer this book to our readers; however, the story, the experiences, and the words are the authors alone. The conversations in the book all come from the author's recollections, not word-for-word transcripts. All of the events are true to the best of the author's memory. The author, in no way, represents any company, corporation, or brand mentioned herein. The views expressed are solely those of the author.

Scripture quotations marked, (NLT) are taken from the *Holy Bible*, New Living Translation, copyright ©1996, 2004, 2015 by Tyndale House Foundation. Used by permission of Tyndale House Publishers, Carol Stream, Illinois 60188. All rights reserved.

Scripture quotations marked, (NIV) are taken from the Holy Bible, New International Version®, NIV®. Copyright © 1973, 1978, 1984, 2011 by Biblica, Inc.™ Used by permission of Zondervan. All rights reserved worldwide. www.zondervan.com The "NIV" and "New International Version" are trademarks registered in the United States Patent and Trad3emark Office by Biblica, Inc.™

DEDICATION

We would like to dedicate this book to Devon and Dray Ely for being amazing sons and grandsons. We love you and are so proud of the young men and leaders you are becoming. Keep leading, keep serving, and keep loving those around you.

PRAISE FOR LEADERSHIP REBORN

"From timeless biblical principles to relatable modern-day examples, *Leadership Reborn* skillfully explains that faith in God is the fuel to lead with maximum impact, no matter the size of your scope or mission. Larry and Daniel clearly articulate that faith isn't simply an essential element of leadership but is designed to be its foundation."

TIM EHRHART: INTERNATIONAL MISSIONS STRATEGIST
HIGH SCHOOL MINISTRY, CRU

"If you are a leader and desire to lead well, do yourself a favor and read *Leadership Reborn*. Larry and Daniel pull examples from biblical heroes and leaders throughout history to encourage and inspire you in your journey. Their practical insights will impact your life and leadership."

TODD PEARAGE: FOUNDER AND DIRECTOR
YOUTH LEADER OASIS

"Well done, Larry and Daniel, for giving us a book that is perfect for the times we are living in right now. If you want to lead from a deep faith perspective, then this book is for you. I can't wait for you to get your hands on this book and implement these truths into your everyday life; you and I will be better for it."

MARK N. SHANER: SOUTHEAST REGIONAL COORDINATOR
NATIONAL NETWORK OF YOUTH MINISTRIES

"I like this book! It is plain talk drawn from the stories of eight strong leaders in the Bible, including Jesus, and is filled with practical illustrations and cautions from today. The convincing argument is to center our lives and leadership strategies on our faith in our Lord. There is a logical progression of lessons, candor about how hard leadership is, and great application questions. You will like it and benefit!"

KNUTE LARSON: PASTORAL COACH
PASTOR EMERITUS, THE CHAPEL

"*Leadership Reborn* shows how the spiritual dimension of leadership can not only make you a more effective and healthier leader but also bring true transformation to the lives of those you lead. If you truly want to lead well, then I highly recommend this book; it's a great resource for all aspects of leadership."

BO BOSHERS: PRESIDENT
LEAD222

"The world could certainly benefit from more servant leaders grounded in the ideals of faith, and this book provides a practical roadmap to reflect upon that purposeful journey."

JOHN M. WEIGAND: MD
GERIATRICIAN AND PUBLIC HEALTH ADVOCATE

"Faith-based leadership is a discipline that has not been commonly practiced among companies, churches, or groups as a means of successfully accomplishing intended goals. The authors clearly define what this highly effective form of leadership is and give examples from biblical times to the 21st century. This book should open the eyes of people who are looking to achieve leadership goals but do not know quite how to get there."

THOMAS ADKINS: OIL & GAS ATTORNEY

CONTENTS

INTRODUCTION	1
PART 1 LEADERSHIP BASICS	**5**
1. WHY FAITH-BASED LEADERSHIP?	7
PART 2 FAITH CHANGES OUR LEADERSHIP	**17**
2. CHANGE IN MOTIVATION: Why Lead? *(David)*	19
3. CHANGE IN PURPOSE: What's the Goal? *(Joshua)*	37
4. CHANGE IN VALUES: What's Important? *(Jesus)*	53
5. CHANGE IN STRATEGY: What's the Plan? *(Nehemiah)*	67
6. CHANGE IN POWER: Who's in Charge? *(Abraham)*	83
7. CHANGE IN PERSPECTIVE: What Matters Most *(Joseph)*	99
8. CHANGE IN OUTCOMES: How Do You Succeed? *(Paul)*	115
9. CHANGE IN CREDIT: Who Gets the Glory? *(Moses)*	133
PART 3 ENEMIES TO FAITH-BASED LEADERSHIP	**149**
10. THE ENEMY OF OUR FAITH *(Satan)*	151
11. THE ENEMY'S DOMAIN: The World *(Satan)*	165
12. THE ENEMY WITHIN *(Adam)*	181
13. VICTORY OVER THE ENEMY *(You)*	193
PART 4 LEADING WITH FAITH	**205**
14. THE ART OF LEADING WELL	207
ABOUT THE AUTHORS	221
INDEX OF STORIES	229
ACKNOWLEDGMENTS	231
NOTES	233

INTRODUCTION

Leading others is challenging. It can be hard to figure out the best way to lead and to do it well. With all the busyness and stress that comes with leadership, it can be difficult to keep our faith central. Can you relate to some of the following struggles that leaders face?

In today's culture, many church leaders are struggling to lead their ministries and teams well at a time when the needs of the community are very high, and people are hurting. Business leaders are struggling to manage profit, people, and principles in a success-driven culture. Educators are struggling to lead their schools and students well with limited funding and high expectations. Parents are wrestling with how to lead their kids and families well in a biblically hostile world. Coaches and players are finding it difficult to lead their teams well when the pressure to win is so high and individual player success threatens to pull the team apart. Students are struggling to lead their peers well when popularity, social media, and the stress of life rub against their faith. All of these struggles make it hard for the everyday leader to navigate how to integrate their faith into their leadership.

As authors, we have been church leaders, business leaders, educators, parents, coaches, and students, and we know how challenging it is to lead well. Leading well is hard work with many obstacles, but it is possible to lead with faith and to overcome these challenges. We empathize with those of you on the front lines of leadership, and in the leadership trenches, trying to keep Christ at the center of your lives.

Would you like to become an even better leader and improve your leadership, enhance your effectiveness, and increase your impact with a faith-centered approach? We hope you do because this book is full of practical principles on leading well that relate to your leadership within your company, team, church, school, or family. Investing in your own leadership development is a great decision with huge benefits for you and the people around you.

INTRODUCTION

We're guessing you are probably involved in some type of leadership role; so, let's find out. What kinds of official or unofficial leadership roles do you have? Are you a teacher, business person, church leader, student leader, athlete, coach, parent, shift supervisor, healthcare professional, first responder, engineer, musician, gamer, designer, or restaurant manager? Maybe you lead in other ways, which is great. Regardless of your role, we are excited you are on the leadership journey. We are grateful that you want to improve your leadership with a faith-based approach. In case no one has told you lately, thank you for all the ways you lead others.

We will cover a lot of leadership ground over the course of this book. Hopefully, you will be able to learn, grow, and apply some of the leadership principles that we will discuss. However, it takes time and experience to lead well, and chances are you can't do it all at once. So, don't try to do it all right away. Break the book down into smaller manageable parts and pick an area on which to focus. Whether you are reading this book on your own or as a group, work on developing each aspect of your leadership and then move on to another area, principle, or chapter.

This isn't a one-size-fits-all type of book. While many of the leadership concepts are universal and unchanging, adapt the principles to fit your leadership context and use the discussion questions to think through and customize the application of those principles. For example, the principle of serving others won't change, but the way we serve and how we serve will look different depending on your leadership role and context.

Leadership Reborn: 8 Ways Faith Transforms Your Everyday Leadership will help transform your leadership with very practical principles on leading well that translate into the real world of coaching, running a company, parenting, serving in the church, leading a business meeting, serving on student council, teaching at a school, working at a restaurant, helping others in the community, or playing on the sports field. To that end, we will take an in-depth look at the leadership of others including:

- **10 LEADERS** from the Bible
- **10 STORIES** illustrating leadership principles
- **10 SPOTLIGHTS** highlighting leadership in action
- **10+ QUOTES** from interviews with leaders
- **80+ QUESTIONS** to discuss and help you grow

Let's be real for a moment. Are you the best leader you can be? Do you think you can improve your leadership? Who would benefit if you became an even better leader than you already are? What role does faith play in your current style of leadership? What would it take for you to embrace faith as the central element of your leadership?

Hopefully, those questions got your mind going. For now, let's back up for a moment and take a look at leadership from a more traditional perspective.

THE VALUE OF TRADITIONAL MODELS

The field of leadership is full of some amazing people, authors, ideas, concepts, and models. If you have a heart to learn, there is no shortage of materials and resources to practically improve your leadership. From authors like John Maxwell, Stephen and Sean Covey, and Bill George, to Tony Dungy, Simon Sinek, and Daniel Goleman, we have been given many great leadership laws, principles, habits, theories, styles, types, and techniques. The topic of leadership is expansive and diverse, from professional strategies to personal growth.

Many of these leadership authors and experts have made very valuable contributions to the field of leadership and have helped many people and companies improve their overall leadership. In particular, I think that principle-centered, others-centered, and values-based leadership models resonate with my own leadership style and fit well with the leadership perspective of this book. However, I think these models would benefit from a faith-based approach which would improve people's leadership even more.

Traditional models can be helpful in framing important leadership principles, developing skills, recognizing pitfalls, and helping leaders identify where and how their leadership style works best. Leadership can assume many forms depending on management

INTRODUCTION

style, organizational size, hierarchical structure, long- and short-term goals, and many other factors. Because the field of leadership is so vast, there are many different approaches to what works best in various leadership contexts.

Here is a brief overview of some common styles of leadership:

- **Authoritarian:** Do it my way
- **Democratic:** Group input and general consensus
- **Diplomatic:** Common ground and peacemaking
- **Transactional:** Give something and get something
- **Servant:** Others first
- **Utilitarian:** People are a means to an end
- **Bureaucratic:** By the book
- **Collaborative:** Teamwork and goal focused
- **Coaching:** People development
- **Laissez-faire:** Hands-off approach
- **Transformational:** Cast vision and push change [1] [2]

While each style or philosophy has its strengths and weaknesses, some forms of leadership are better than others. For example, while an authoritarian approach can work well in the military or in crisis situations, it tends to breed employee dissatisfaction in the business workplace and frustrates children and teenagers as a parenting model. While traditional leadership styles and models can be very helpful in understanding leadership and developing leaders, there is more to leading well than many of these approaches address. There is a spiritual dimension to leadership that often goes overlooked or ignored. The rest of this book is devoted to exploring this missing element. So, let's jump right in!

PART 1

LEADERSHIP BASICS

CHAPTER 1
WHY FAITH-BASED LEADERSHIP?

Leadership is like a solar system. Often, there is a central idea or principle that all the other aspects of leadership orbit around. Many organizations have core elements central to their philosophy and approach to leadership. How about you? What central idea, concept, or value does your leadership tend to revolve around?

Before the 1500s, the predominant thinking about the solar system was that the Earth was at the center *(geocentric)*. From the philosophies and mathematics of Aristotle and Ptolemy, people had developed an earth-centered view of astronomy. While many people believed the planets and the sun orbited the Earth, it was incorrect. As a result, having the wrong center led to wrong scientific conclusions. It wasn't until advancements in technology allowed people like Copernicus and Galileo to make observations and calculations that led to the discovery of the sun being the center of the solar system *(heliocentric)*. This was an important shift in how people viewed the stars and planets. As a result, it led to a more accurate understanding of the universe. Having the correct center made all the difference.[3]

In a similar way, having the right center for our leadership makes all the difference. More specifically, a faith-centered approach to leadership makes a huge difference in the way we lead and is the key to leading well. Faith changes our leadership from a self-centered earthly model to a faith-centered heavenly model. We cannot change the fact that the planets in our solar system orbit the sun, but we can

Chapter 1

change what's at the center of our lives and our leadership. When the Son is at the center of our leadership, everything changes.

WHY WE NEED FAITH-BASED LEADERSHIP

Faith makes your leadership better and changes the way you lead in eight fundamental ways that can improve your everyday leadership within your church, company, team, school, and family. How? For starters, a faith-centered approach to leadership changes the way we lead by adding a spiritual engine to the core of our leadership. There is a BIG difference between having faith as one of many principles that guide our leadership and having faith at the center of our leadership infusing all aspects of how we lead.

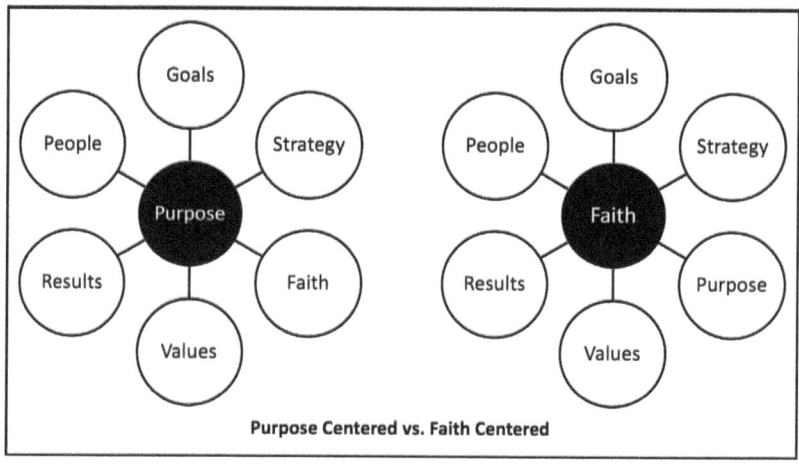

Purpose Centered vs. Faith Centered

At first glance, the purpose-centered model seems like a good approach. Drop whatever your company, team, or group purpose is into the middle and you're off to make money, make food, win games, achieve goals, or make a difference. In this model, your faith may assist you, but it is not the driving force, and it does not inform the other areas of your leadership. The first model works to varying degrees, but there is a better approach.

Think of it like a car engine. The difference between having faith as one of many principles and having faith at the center of your leadership is like the difference between running on a two-cylinder engine versus an eight-cylinder engine. A faith-centered approach has more power, acceleration, and torque for the long haul. Why? The reason is that we can often accomplish more with God's strength fueling us, His principles guiding us, and His Spirit empowering us than we can on our own.

What happens when you infuse faith into the topic of leadership and leadership development? The result is that eight major leadership fundamentals change. There is a change in: motivation, purpose, values, strategy, power, perspective, outcomes, and credit. Faith-based leadership embraces a new set of anchor points that differs from traditional leadership models. Faith makes our leadership better. A faith-centered approach transforms our leadership with:

- A divine motivation and purpose
- A *reprioritizing* of values
- A *reforming* of effective strategies
- A *releasing* of power
- A *renewed* sense of perspective
- A *redefined* view of success
- A *redistribution* of credit

This is leadership REBORN.

Chapter 1

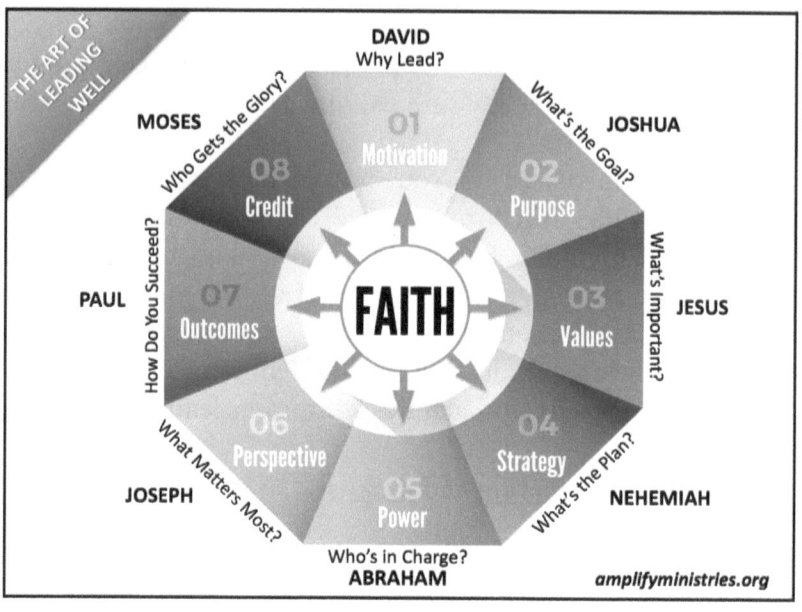

The diagram above shows what it looks like to have our faith infuse all aspects of our leadership. When our faith is at the center of our leadership, it fuels our motivation, purpose, values, and strategy, and it shapes our view of power, perspective, outcomes, and credit.

THE STRUGGLE OF MANY MODELS

The first reason we need faith-based leadership is because many models put other things at the center of their leadership. Many traditional models are driven by performance, economics, personality, goals, purpose, or have other metrics at the center. While many traditional leadership models can be effective, having a faith-based approach can make our leadership even better. Granted, putting faith at the center of some models may cause them to break, but that's not a bad thing. For example, if profit was at the center of your model, then faith might challenge that philosophy and cause you to restructure your leadership, and that's a good thing. Keep profit important but move it out of the center and allow faith to guide where profit fits in your model. In fact, doing that might even make you more profitable or at the very least, a better leader.

Second, most traditional leadership models don't address the problem of human nature. The nature of people is an incredibly challenging obstacle to leading others. The reality is that human nature tends to resist good leadership, whether we are battling our own nature or the nature of the people we lead. Left unchecked, our selfishness taints everything we think and do. Often, traditional models don't adequately deal with the problem of people's innate shortcomings, hidden desires, and poor behavior. Some models address the symptoms with disciplinary actions but lack the ability to deal with the darkness in people's hearts. However, a faith-based approach is uniquely able to handle the problem of corruption at its source; more on that later.

Third, many traditional models can be difficult to sustain. For example, if serving others or servant leadership is one of your leadership values, there is a limit to how long we can serve others well before our selfish nature kicks in and we grow weary of putting others first. Even the best leaders with the best intentions grow tired of serving when they rely on their own strength. However, infusing faith into our leadership changes the equation and we are able to serve longer and better as our faith in God gives us strength and the proper perspective. In this way, our faith can elevate and sustain our leadership in a way that traditional models cannot.

WHAT IS FAITH-BASED LEADERSHIP?

Faith-based leadership is a personal leadership model, but it can also be a company or team model. For example, you can still lead well and have a faith-based approach to leading even if the company you work for does not. The flip side is also true; you can use a faith-based leadership model for your company or team even if everyone who works there does not. While there is a difference between the leadership model of a company or organization and the personal model of leadership that a person is committed to following, both can benefit from having a faith-based approach.

The field of faith-based leadership is full of some amazing people and authors as well. From authors like Tim Elmore, Ken Blanchard, C. Gene Wilkes, to Andy Stanley, Craig Groeschel, and Doug Fields, we have been given many great faith-based leadership principles, habits, attitudes, models, concepts, and strategies. All of

Chapter 1

these leadership authors and experts have made significant contributions to the field of faith-based leadership and have helped countless people, churches, ministries, and companies improve their leadership.

Faith-based leadership is a biblical approach that begins with making God the leader of your life. While putting your faith in God doesn't guarantee that you will be a great leader, it is certainly a strong foundation on which to build great leadership. By putting yourself under God's leadership of your life, it puts you in a position not only to receive great leadership from Him, but to offer it to others as well. While you can be an effective leader without God in your life, you cannot be the best leader you can be.

Just to be clear, faith in God doesn't solve every leadership problem. There are some really bad church leaders and leaders of faith that have stunk up the leadership landscape, many of whom would benefit from a crash course in proper leadership protocols. Faith-based leaders mess up. It's embarrassing, but it's true; many have missed the mark and hurt those around them. In contrast, there are some really good leaders that don't care about God or faith that have made a positive impact in the world. What's the point? The point is that faith merely opens the door for better leadership. You still have to choose to walk through it and develop yourself into a better leader.

The best leaders are those who have put their faith in Christ and allow their faith to infuse their leadership. Why? Well, the reason has to do with our corrupt nature and the corruption in the world. Without Jesus as the leader of your life, most of the leadership principles in this book will be extremely difficult, if not impossible, to do on your own. Your human nature will fight against this type of leadership, and it won't work for very long. The bottom line is this: you have to have God energizing and empowering you to make these changes in your leadership because they are not normal or natural.

If that resonates with you, great! If that bothers you, that's okay too. We understand. We just want to be completely upfront with where we are going. But hold on; keep reading. There is a lot more this book has to offer. Keep an open mind and you might be surprised at how your leadership might benefit from a faith-based perspective. No matter where you are on your leadership and faith journey, we believe this book will be incredibly practical and that people from all walks of life and faith can gain something useful along the way.

A WHOLE-PERSON APPROACH TO LEADERSHIP

Another reason we need a faith-based view is because leading well requires a whole-person approach to leadership that involves all four aspects of a person: heart, mind, body, and soul. Check out the following brief descriptions of each core aspect and how they relate to our leadership.

The Character of a Leader (Heart)

The character of a leader is who you are on the inside. Are you a moral and ethical person? Do you live and lead with integrity? Do you have a good heart and pure motives? Do you lead with noble values and principles? Are you a good role model for others? Do you have character flaws? Do you take steps to guard and protect your character? Is there anything in your life that helps keep your heart in check and on track? Do you have healthy boundaries in your life for your personal conduct? Do you do things that build up your character in positive ways?

The Thinking of a Leader (Mind)

The thinking of a leader is about your mindset, thoughts, and perspective. Do you give careful thought and attention to your leadership? Have you thought things through? Are you intentional, purposeful, and strategic in your planning? Do you compare and contrast the pros and cons? Do you consider the consequences, costs, and benefits to others in your decision-making? Do you evaluate and analyze the best options? Do you seek the wisdom of others to guide your thinking and choices? What or who is at the center of your thinking? Do you find ways to renew your mind and gain the proper perspective?

Chapter 1

The Actions of a Leader (Body)

The actions of a leader are how we actually lead and what we actually do. Our actions flow out of our hearts, minds, and souls. Do you lead by example? Do you consistently take action, accomplish tasks, and do what is needed? Are you involved in the regular activity of your team? Are you productive with your time and energy? Are you lazy or apathetic? Do you procrastinate or are you slow to act? Do you communicate well with your team? Do you show people the how and why of what is required of them? Do you set goals for your team and help them succeed? Do you inspire, motivate, and cast vision? Do you build others up? Do you train? Do you serve? Do you actually lead?

The Faith of a Leader (Soul)

The faith of a leader is the spiritual aspect of a person that fuels and guides the heart, mind, and body. If we remove or ignore the faith part of our lives and leadership, we lose an important dimension of who we are and how we were meant to lead. Is faith in God important to you? Do you allow your faith to infuse your leadership? Is faith at the center of how you lead, informing and guiding all the other aspects of your leadership? Do you rely on God for strength, wisdom, and guidance? Do you do things to feed your soul and invest in your own spiritual growth? Do you care about the spiritual health and well-being of the people you lead?

How They Work Together

Now, let's bring it all together. The art of leading well requires a whole-person approach to leadership because each core aspect of a person's being is essential. If we neglect one part or another, we limit the reach and depth of our leadership. For example, if we neglect the *heart* of a leader and have poor character, people are going to lose trust in us because we lack integrity or a moral center. If we neglect the *mind* and don't think thoughtfully, strategically, and have the right mindset, people won't know what the plan is or why they are doing it. If we neglect the *body* and don't take any action as a leader, people are not going to want to follow us because we are not accomplishing or engaging in things. If we neglect the *soul* and the faith of a leader, our leadership is left without a vital power source that fuels, guides, and protects the heart, mind, and body. All four aspects work together in synchrony and are affected by the others to create harmony or discord depending on how we cultivate them. As a result, faith-based leadership better equips us to lead people because it addresses the whole person: heart, mind, body, and soul.

WRAP UP

Hopefully, you have a better understanding of faith-based leadership and why we need it. While faith-based leadership does not solve every leadership issue, it does provide an amazing foundation on which to build great leadership. There is a lot we can learn from leaders of faith and how they put their faith and their leadership into practice.

Coming up next in part two: we'll cover the eight leadership fundamentals that change when we infuse our leadership with faith. From Adam to Jesus, we will take a look at key principles from biblical leaders and how we can implement the good and avoid their mistakes.

In addition, we have some great stories and spotlights for you to look forward to, including: Olympic snowboarding, trips to outer space, government conspiracies, corporate infighting, football parties, soccer championships, daring rescues, incredible inventions, assassinations, reality shows, animated cartoons, military combat, and chicken sandwiches.

Chapter 1

PUTTING IT INTO PRACTICE

Before you move on, think about, discuss, and apply the following questions as they relate to your leadership within your company, team, church, school, or family.

Leadership Thoughts

1. What are some of your current official and unofficial leadership roles?
2. Have you ever experienced good leadership? What made it good?
3. Have you ever experienced bad leadership? What made it bad?
4. What are some of your strengths and weaknesses as a leader?
5. Who would benefit if you became an even better leader than you already are?
6. What role does faith play in your current style of leadership?
7. What would it take for you to embrace faith as the central element of your leadership?
8. How would you rate or describe your current leadership in regard to your: heart (character), mind (thinking), body (actions), and soul (faith)?

PART 2

FAITH CHANGES OUR LEADERSHIP

CHAPTER 2
CHANGE IN MOTIVATION:
Why Lead?
Featured Leader: David

Good food is a great motivator. In fact, football season is not the same without good food. Pizza, seven-layer nacho dip, wings, chips, drinks, and a big-screen TV are all the makings of a great party. Add some friends, dance music, and homemade desserts to the mix, and everybody is ready for game time. Whether you show up to the party for the snacks, the friends, the game, the commercials, or all of the above, football parties are fun!

A group of us had gathered at a friend's house to watch the big game and hang out. It was Super Bowl 45, and the Green Bay Packers were playing the Pittsburgh Steelers. I was excited to cheer on the Packers and was wearing my lucky Reggie White jersey #92. On TV, the stands were full of fans sporting foam cheese-heads chanting "Go! Pack! Go!" and pumping their fists to motivate their team. It was a fun game to watch. As the food disappeared, the score went up. My friends and I cheered as the Packers won the game by six. The victory was a cause for celebration and motivated a fair amount of friendly taunting toward the Steelers fans in the room.[4]

I first became a Packers fan when I heard Reggie White give a motivational message at a conference. I was inspired by him as a player because he held the all-time leading sack record for a long time with 198 sacks as a defensive end.[5] I was also inspired by his leadership and his faith as an ordained minister.

Chapter 2

After reading his book, I connected with his journey as a player and pastor, and I appreciated the team's rich history. It was easy to become a fan with legendary coach Vince Lombardi, historic Lambeau Field, and quarterbacks Brett Favre and Aaron Rodgers leading the way. My high school football coach often quoted Coach Lombardi in order to motivate our team and posted inspirational sayings around the locker room and in our playbooks.

Actually, Vince Lombardi is considered one of the greatest motivators in football history. He is well known for leading the Packers to their first two NFL Championships in Super Bowl I and II, and the Super Bowl trophy is even named after him. According to his son and his players, Lombardi was a master motivator and knew how to motivate his team and inspire his players.[4]

> *"Motivation is not a one-step fix…. You need to create momentum, through short-term wins that give credibility and staying power to your vision…. The goal of winning the championship, therefore, had to be built on the foundation of a thousand small victories. It depended on each player seeing the connection between his individual effort and winning the championship."* [6]

Vince Lombardi knew that there were external factors and internal factors that motivate people and players. He often used positive and negative reinforcement with his team. He could be harsh and offensive and would sometimes get up in a player's face, but he could also be compassionate and caring for the lives of his men. All in all, he knew deep down that the key to motivation was in a person's heart.

> *"I believe it is essential to understand that battles are won primarily in the <u>hearts</u> of men. Men respond to leadership in a most remarkable way. Once you have won their <u>hearts</u>, they will follow you anywhere."* [7] (emphasis added)

If that's true, and I believe it is, then what happens when we apply it to leadership and faith? Perhaps it looks something like this: "When God wins your heart, you will follow him anywhere." When we give our hearts to God, it changes us and it changes our leadership. There is now a divine motivation to follow God, to lead, and to help others. As our motivations and reasons for leading begin to take on new meaning, there becomes a spiritual aspect to our leadership and our leadership roles.

While sometimes God calls us to lead for a specific purpose, often our motivations are not spiritual. People lead for all different kinds of reasons. Maybe someone is asked to lead so they step up. Maybe there is a vacancy or a job posting so they apply. Sometimes, the need to lead is clear because no one is doing it. Other times, people are voted into leadership or assigned a leadership role. Often, someone steps down from leadership and another person takes over. Occasionally, leaders emerge in a group because the group lacks direction or focus. Motivations for leading vary widely from personal gain to helping others. Usually, our motivations to lead follow our passions. What motivates you to lead?

Personally, my motivations for leading have ranged all over from being asked to lead by teachers and coaches to being voted into leadership roles by peers. I have been assigned teams of people to supervise and manage at work, and I have taken on leadership roles to get a paycheck. I have applied for leadership positions in order to help others, and I have been motivated by God's calling on my life to lead.

Chapter 2

I am not a leadership expert, but I have had a fair amount of experience and have learned a lot about leadership over the years as a:

- Director
- Manager
- Supervisor
- Student Pastor
- Teacher
- Speaker
- Counselor
- Consultant
- Author
- Coach
- Team Captain
- Committee Member
- Eagle Scout
- Volunteer
- Husband
- Father

I am passionate about the need for better leaders and better leadership. Leading well begins with the right motivations and having the right heart. When a leader's heart and motives are in the right place, good things tend to happen. However, when a leader's motives are suspect and his or her heart is in the wrong place, poor leadership emerges, people get hurt, and bad things are on the horizon.

The Bible is full of good and bad leaders, corrupt kings and righteous servants, leaders with pure motives, and ones with dark agendas. David was one of the good ones. Most of the time, David was an honorable leader and man after the heart of God.

DAVID'S HEART

There are foundational leadership principles that we can learn from the life of David and his heart for God. We can see these principles in key ways as he was <u>called</u> to lead, how he was <u>committed</u> to God, when he was <u>challenged</u> to give up, as he was <u>confirmed</u> as king, and how he was <u>contrite</u> and open-hearted when he made mistakes.

LEADERSHIP REBORN

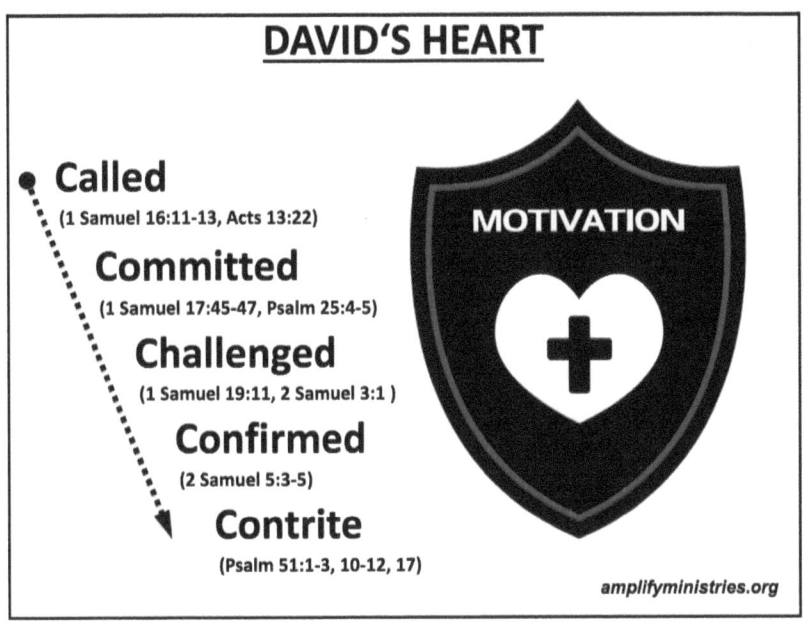

CALLED TO LEAD

If a friend or someone important asked you to take a leadership role, would you do it? It might depend on the person, the position, the pay, or the time commitment, but most of us would probably give it some serious consideration. What if God was the one inviting you to lead? Would you accept? If you are like me, you would probably have lots of questions before making a decision. Is God's calling enough to motivate you to action? It was for a young shepherd named David.

David was called to lead at a young age, most likely as a teenager. He was not the oldest, fastest, or strongest, but he was chosen over his older brothers to be a leader. While he was tending the sheep God called him and had him anointed to become the future king of Israel. God saw potential in him and knew he had the right heart to eventually lead His people.

> Then Samuel asked, "Are these all the sons you have?" "There is still the youngest," Jesse replied. "But he's out in the fields watching the sheep and goats." "Send for

Chapter 2

him at once," Samuel said. "We will not sit down to eat until he arrives." So Jesse sent for him. He was dark and handsome, with beautiful eyes. And the LORD said, "This is the one; anoint him." So as David stood there among his brothers, Samuel took the flask of olive oil he had brought and anointed David with the oil. And the Spirit of the LORD came powerfully upon David from that day on.... (1 Samuel 16:11-13, NLT)

After removing Saul, he made David their king. God testified concerning him: 'I have found David son of Jesse, a man after my own heart; he will do everything I want him to do.' (Acts 13:22, NIV)

Although David was called to leadership early in his life, he did not become king right away. His leadership journey was a long one and his rise to leadership took a significant amount of time. What's important at the beginning is why he was chosen. He feared and followed the Lord, and his heart was in the right place. This set David apart from his brothers because God knew that he could do great things through a person whose heart was devoted to Him. What's more, God called him to lead and David answered and embraced that calling.

Faith-based leadership begins with an open heart toward God and a willingness to follow His leading in our lives. How will you respond, or how have you responded to God when prompted to lead or take a leadership role?

COMMITTED TO GOD

One of the best things about David was his commitment to God. We see his devotion to the Lord early in his life when he went to check on his three oldest brothers who were serving in King Saul's army. Israel was facing off against the Philistine army in the valley of Elah.

When David arrived on the battlefront to bring supplies, he saw the giant Philistine champion standing about nine feet tall and wearing bronze armor. David heard Goliath taunting and insulting the Israelite forces, and he was bothered that no one went out to silence the enemy's threats against God's people. Saul and his men were afraid, but not David.

Driven by his passionate and committed faith in God, David decided to do battle against Goliath himself. Armed with only a sling and some stones, David attacked the giant, and God gave him victory over Goliath. David's courage and faith gave the Israelite forces the motivation they needed.

> *David replied to the Philistine, "You come to me with sword, spear, and javelin, but I come to you in the name of the LORD of Heaven's Armies—the God of the armies of Israel, whom you have defied. Today the LORD will conquer you, and I will kill you and cut off your head. And then I will give the dead bodies of your men to the birds and wild animals, and the whole world will know that there is a God in Israel! And everyone assembled here will know that the LORD rescues his people, but not with sword and spear. This is the LORD's battle, and he will give you to us!"*
> (1 Samuel 17:45-47, NLT)

Motivated by his faith, God's calling on his life, and the possibility of reward if he survived, David inspired the troops and gained favor with the king. David stepped up to the challenge when no one else did, and he trusted God to give him victory in battle when all the odds were stacked against him. With the giant defeated, the Israelite forces chased down the Philistine soldiers and routed their army.

Another example of David's deep commitment to the Lord can be found in the book of Psalms. David's heart, love for God, and deep faith can be seen over and over again as he worships, writes songs, and sings throughout the Psalms. He often worships God for his faithfulness, love, salvation, and protection and laments to God about his pain, fear, sin, and sorrow.

Chapter 2

> *Show me your ways, LORD, teach me your paths. Guide me in your truth and teach me, for you are God my Savior, and my hope is in you all day long. (Psalm 25:4-5, NIV)*

As king, we also see David's commitment to the Lord. One of the major things David did to restore Israel was to bring back the Ark of the Covenant to Jerusalem. David, his troops, and the people of Israel retrieved it and set it up in a special place of honor. Then, David worshipped God, offered sacrifices to the Lord, and blessed the people. By doing all these things, David brought the importance of worshiping God to front and center. He made it abundantly clear to all the people he was leading that worship was central.

> *So David went there and brought the Ark of God from the house of Obed-edom to the City of David with a great celebration.... So David and all the people of Israel brought up the Ark of the LORD with shouts of joy and the blowing of rams' horns.*
> *(2 Samuel 6:12b, 15, NLT)*

David's commitment to follow God for the long haul set him apart as a strong leader. Leading well starts with the leader's heart. Having a heart that is solely committed to God and devoted to the Lord makes all the difference when it comes to leading others. We can't lead well if our hearts are in the wrong place. We must push aside our selfish desires, resist the things that distract our hearts, and be steadfast in our commitment to God above all else.

CHALLENGED TO GIVE UP

David's road to becoming king was long and difficult. It was filled with many roadblocks and significant obstacles that blocked his path time and time again. Enemies, division, assassination attempts, and war, all threatened to undermine David and end his life or cause him to give up.

One of David's biggest enemies was the king himself. David found great favor with King Saul at first, but over time the king became jealous of David's popularity and grew to hate him. Saul hunted David on several occasions and tried to have him killed.

Then Saul sent troops to watch David's house. They were told to kill David when he came out the next morning... (1 Samuel 19:11a, NLT)

David stayed in the wilderness strongholds and in the hills of the Desert of Ziph. Day after day Saul searched for him, but God did not give David into his hands. While David was at Horesh in the Desert of Ziph, he learned that Saul had come out to take his life. (1 Samuel 23:14-15, NIV)

God promised David he would become king of Israel, but God's timing remained a mystery. For a long time, David's path to the throne was blocked. Someone else was the King of Israel. First, Saul was king, and later Saul's son Ish-Bosheth was promoted and made King of Israel instead of David. Over time, David was made king of the tribe of Judah, but he had to continue to wait seven more years to become King of Israel.

Ish-Bosheth son of Saul was forty years old when he became king over Israel, and he reigned two years. The tribe of Judah, however, remained loyal to David. (2 Samuel 2:10, NIV)

War blocked David's path. The tension between the house of Saul and the house of David grew into an all-out war. As the fighting raged on, David's favor, position, and strength grew as his armies slowly achieved victory battle after battle.

The war between the house of Saul and the house of David lasted a long time. David grew stronger and

Chapter 2

stronger, while the house of Saul grew weaker and weaker. (2 Samuel 3:1, NIV)

In order to paint a clearer picture of what David was up against, here is a summary of some major roadblocks to becoming King.

ROADBLOCKS TO THE THRONE

OPEN ROAD: God calls and promises David he will be king
   ROADBLOCK #1: Someone else was King (Saul)

OPEN ROAD: Saul likes David and gives him a high rank
   ROADBLOCK #2: Saul is jealous of David and tries to kill him

OPEN ROAD: God protects David
   ROADBLOCK #3: David has to wait on God's timing

OPEN ROAD: King Saul dies
   ROADBLOCK #4: Saul's commander turns against David

OPEN ROAD: David is made king over a small area (Judah)
   ROADBLOCK #5: Ish-Bosheth is made king (Saul's son)

OPEN ROAD: David continues to rely on God and trust Him
   ROADBLOCK #6: War and years of fighting

OPEN ROAD: Ish-Bosheth is killed, and David is made king of Israel

The roadblocks in David's life continually challenged him to give up and abandon his leadership journey and God's calling on his life. The temptations to quit, to stop, to hide, to retreat, and to accept defeat were strong, yet he stood firm and resisted. God was with David, and he managed to push ahead despite incredible opposition.

Leading well requires a certain tenacity and grit in the face of opposition. It takes strong faith and bold determination to hold your ground, to plow ahead one difficult step at a time, and to take on the obstacles that block our path. Many leaders turn back, decide it is not worth it, or abandon the quest for an easier road. At times, I have been tempted to give up in the face of giant obstacles, oppressive opposition, and formidable challenges that were before me. I felt like I lacked the strength and the faith to continue. Without the faith, friendship, and provision of those around me, I would not have made it.

Faith-based leadership clings to the promises of God in the face of adversity, holds fast to the calling God put in our hearts, locks arms with those around them, and trusts that if God has called us, then he will make a way.

CONFIRMED AS KING

After overcoming many obstacles in his path, David became king of Judah at the age of thirty. He reigned over this smaller region for seven years, before he finally became king of all Israel at the age of thirty-seven. God blessed his kingship as David found favor with the Lord and with the people of Israel. He reigned for a long time and prospered as King until the age of seventy.

> *So there at Hebron, King David made a covenant before the LORD with all the elders of Israel. And they anointed him king of Israel. David was <u>thirty years</u> old when he began to reign, and he reigned forty years in all. He had reigned over Judah from Hebron for seven years and six months, and from Jerusalem he reigned over all Israel and Judah for thirty-three years. (2 Sam. 5:3-5 NLT, emphasis added)*

David's confirmation as king of Judah and Israel points to God's faithfulness over time. God called him to leadership and now after years of preparation and perseverance, his official role had begun. I am guessing that his family had their doubts about it when he was initially anointed king by Samuel, but God delivered on his promise. David's heart for God opened the door for God to use him in some amazing ways. As a result, the nation of Israel prospered under David's rule. Leading well starts with having a heart for God, and then it embraces the leadership opportunities God brings along.

Chapter 2

CONTRITE AND OPEN-HEARTED

Although David made many mistakes in his life and messed up publicly as a leader at times, he remained committed to his faith. He continued to be open-hearted toward God, and contrite about his sins. One of David's biggest mistakes as king was that he slept with another man's wife and had him killed in battle to cover it up. It can be a bit perplexing to reconcile how a man guilty of adultery and murder can be called a man after God's heart. Those actions were wrong and sinful, and he was punished for them. Clearly, his heart went astray for a time. However, there is much more to David than his sins. When confronted with his shortcomings, David confessed, repented, and kept a soft heart toward God.

> *Have mercy on me, O God, because of your unfailing love. Because of your great compassion, blot out the stain of my sins. Wash me clean from my guilt. Purify me from my sin. For I recognize my rebellion; it haunts me day and night. (Psalm 51:1-3, NLT)*

> *Create in me a <u>pure heart</u>, O God, and renew a steadfast spirit within me. Do not cast me from your presence or take your Holy Spirit from me. Restore to me the joy of your salvation and grant me a willing spirit, to sustain me. (Psalm 51:10-12 NIV, emphasis added)*

What made David a great leader was his heart for God, his faithful devotion to the Lord, and his willingness to continually come back to God when he messed up. David was far from perfect, but he knew that it was not about perfect behavior; it was about having a right heart, a forgiven heart, and a humble heart before God.

> *My sacrifice, O God, is a broken spirit; a broken and <u>contrite heart</u> you, God, will not despise. (Psalm 51:17 NIV, emphasis added)*

> *Above all else, guard your <u>heart</u>, for everything you do flows from it. (Proverbs 4:23 NIV, emphasis added)*

Faith-based leadership involves surrendering your heart to God and then protecting your heart from going astray. Leading well over the course of time requires a diligent guarding of our hearts that involves repeatedly focusing and refocusing on the Lord. It takes hard work, a disciplined mind, lots of prayers, good friends, regular doses of God's word, a spirit of worship, and a sensitivity to the things of God to keep our hearts and our motivations on track and out of trouble.

THE CHANGE: Motivation + Faith

How does infusing faith into our leadership affect our motivation? Faith reframes our motivation, why we lead, and how we motivate others in three key ways.

First, leading well starts with the leader's heart. Faith-based leadership begins with an open heart toward God and a willingness to follow His leading in our lives. Leading well invites us to ask God to purify our motives and reasons for leading and to keep our hearts in check and on target. Because it is easy to drift off course, it is essential that our faith anchors our motivations and our hearts to God. Otherwise, we may be responsible for leading others to drift off course as well.

Second, our faith becomes a powerful motivator in our leadership because it adds a spiritual aspect to why we lead. The reason we lead takes on a new meaning. It can turn ordinary motivations for leading others into a divine calling to make a difference for God's kingdom. If you are called to lead, then you need to lead. In addition, faith-based leadership recognizes that God can also give the spiritual gift of leadership to people which can motivate them to lead because of the abilities He has given them (Romans 12:6-8). If you have the gift of leadership, then use it well to help guide, and build up others.

Third, our faith can not only change our motivations for leading, but it can also change how we motivate others. While leading well is often motivated by our faith in God, we can help motivate others by helping them identify their own faith-based reasons for participating and engaging in our leadership vision. Faith-based leadership finds ways to truly motivate and inspire people in noble ways without using intimidation, manipulation, guilt, or fear. Leading well requires us to resist our lower nature and less-than-honorable tactics and elevate the people around us with positive motivational techniques. Again, we are trying to win people's hearts and confidence, and that is done through mutual trust, respect, and pure motives.

LEADERSHIP SPOTLIGHT: JOHN F. KENNEDY AND PT-109

There are times in our leadership roles when things do not go as we planned. Sometimes, it all falls apart and our leadership acumen is stretched to the limit. Dan shares the following true story about John F. Kennedy's unbelievable experience while commanding a Navy patrol torpedo boat.

During WWII, John F. Kennedy (JFK) was a Lieutenant in the Navy. On one of his missions for the US allied forces, he was in command of patrol torpedo boat PT-109. While Lt. Kennedy and his crew were patrolling a group of islands in the South Pacific, their boat was rammed in the night by a Japanese destroyer and sank off the coast of Kolobangara Island in the Solomon Islands on August 2, 1943.[8]

Heart to Help His Men

With his boat smashed to pieces and sinking, Lt. Kennedy gathered his wits and scrambled to save his scattered and injured crew in the midst of the burning chaos. Motivated by survival, a heart for his men, and commitment to his country, Lt. Kennedy helped his crew survive in the water, escape the wreckage, and swim to the nearest island.[8]

Roadblocks and Obstacles

After assessing his crew of 12, two men had died in the initial collision and explosion, and many men were injured. Of the crewmen remaining, some of them were not good swimmers and one man was too injured to swim and had to be towed by the others. Lt. Kennedy had to fight terrific odds to keep his men alive. He and his men were challenged to give up in the face of tremendous obstacles: their boat was sunk, they had very little food or water, they had little to no supplies, they had to evade the enemy who was trying to kill them, they were surrounded by water on a small island chain with no communication, and many of them were hurt.[8]

Determination and Motivation

Relying on his athletic skills from being on the Harvard swim team, Lt. Kennedy went on a series of long swims, two to three miles each, going island to island searching for food and trying to find help with no success. As time went on, his men became discouraged and wanted to surrender to the Japanese boats cruising the area and get food. Determined not to give up, Lt. Kennedy said "no" and motivated his desperate crew to continue to fight to survive. Again, he made another long swim of several miles to try and find help.[9]

On August 4, Lt. Kennedy and Ensign Thom assisted all of their injured and hungry crew on a difficult team swim of 3.75 miles to Olasana Island to search for food. They found coconuts to eat but no fresh water.[9]

Searching and Waiting

On August 5, Lt. Kennedy and another crewman named Ross continued to search for food and help by swimming for an hour to another small island where they found a dugout canoe. It was then that they met the natives of the area and convinced them that they were Americans, not Japanese, and needed help. The natives brought food to them and helped the starving and hurt crewmen.

On August 6, the natives agreed to take a message that Lt. Kennedy etched on a coconut describing their approximate location

Chapter 2

and the number of men in the surviving crew. After their long search for food and aid, Lt. Kennedy and his crew now had to wait for help to come and hope their message would be received.[9]

Rescue and Relief

The natives headed east and canoed 38 miles for 15 hours on the high seas to another island in order to deliver the makeshift S.O.S. After another canoe trip by the natives, a successful message got back to an American PT base at Rendova. Amazingly, the message of the crew's survival was passed along to the right people. Finally, on August 8, after a week of incredible survival, Lt. Kennedy and his crew were rescued.[9]

THE POINT

Crisis tests our leadership and the struggle to survive pushes us to our limits and beyond. In an instant, leadership can be forced upon us, and we have to respond quickly. In the face of overwhelming circumstances, Lt. Kennedy's leadership and determination helped his crew stay alive, stay motivated, and defy the odds. With the help of the natives, they survived and were rescued. While Kennedy's actions as a young lieutenant were not necessarily faith-based, they resemble similar qualities of David's leadership in regard to his heart and commitment to his men, motivating his crew under adverse conditions, being challenged to give up, and overcoming obstacles. Leading well incorporates all these things and often asks more of ourselves than we ever thought possible.

> ## FROM THE TRENCHES
> ### WHAT DOES IT TAKE TO LEAD WELL IN YOUR LEADERSHIP CONTEXT?
>
> "It takes initiative to lead well. It takes the ability to rally and motivate others. A great leader needs to be knowledgeable about their field and not be afraid to do the hard things to get there. Leaders can't please everyone, but they can gain the respect of others by setting a good example and leading with humility."
>
> -Devon Ely
> Senior Intern at Pursuit Aerospace [10]

Chapter 2

PUTTING IT INTO PRACTICE:
What does a change in <u>motivation</u> mean to you?

Before you move on, think about, discuss, and apply the following questions as they relate to your leadership within your company, team, church, school, or family.

Leadership Thoughts

1. What key points stick out to you from this chapter and why?
2. How's your heart? Is it open to God and His leading in your life? Explain.
3. What motivates you to lead, and in what areas do you feel called to leadership?
4. How does infusing faith into your leadership affect your motivation to lead?
5. What are some positive ways you can motivate and inspire the people you lead?
6. What are some of the challenging obstacles that you have faced in your leadership and how did you navigate them?

CHAPTER 3
CHANGE IN PURPOSE:
What's the Goal?
Featured Leader: Joshua

Sometimes things don't go as planned. Life has a way of shifting our goals suddenly and forcing us to adapt to new situations. Dan shares the following story about the change in the purpose of the Apollo 13 space mission.

In April 1970, the Apollo 13 rocket was preparing for launch. It was the seventh mission of the Apollo project, and the third mission designed to land on the moon. The purpose of the mission was to conduct soil analysis, explore the terrain, take lunar photographs, and better understand how people function on the moon. Jim Lovell, Jack Swigert, and Fred Haise were the three astronauts aboard the Apollo 13, and they were excited to get the mission underway. The spacecraft consisted of three modules: the command module, which was the main vehicle; the service module, which housed the oxygen/fuel cells/batteries/life support; and the lunar module, which would take them to the moon's surface. The launch and first day went pretty well, but then things changed.

Two days into the mission, there was a strange reading from one of the oxygen tanks in the service module. Mission Control asked them to stir the oxygen tank to see if that would correct the issue and fix any sensor problems. They heard a loud "bang" and when they looked out the window, they saw gas leaking into space. They quickly reported to Mission Control, "Houston, we have a problem." It was

Chapter 3

determined that an explosion in one of the oxygen tanks had damaged both tanks. As a result, they were losing oxygen which affected life support, water production, and cooling. In addition, they were also losing power. They were not sure why the explosion happened, but now their lives were in danger. At this point, the purpose of the mission completely changed. The situation forced them to shift their goals from exploration and discovery to survival and rescue.

Mission Control made the decision that in order to survive they would need to transfer to the lunar module and use it as a "lifeboat" to get back home. The lunar module was designed to support two men for two days, not three men for four days. With survival as the main goal, they all focused on trying to solve each of the problems that each new decision created. Instead of landing on the moon as part of their original goal, they decided to circle the moon in order to get the right trajectory to return to Earth. This maneuver took valuable time and resources which had already been running low. To make matters worse, the temperature had dropped severely due to the power loss. At one point the temperature dropped to 38°F, the atmosphere was wet, the oxygen and power were low, and carbon dioxide was building up fast.

The explosion had caused the CO_2 scrubbers to quit functioning, causing dangerous levels of toxic gas to rise in the cabin. Even though the lunar module had enough oxygen and fuel for the immediate time, the rising levels of carbon dioxide could cause the crew to suffocate. They needed to figure out a new solution quickly. In the command module, they had some lithium hydroxide which is the chemical used to remove the CO_2. However, they had to modify the container needed in order to use it in the lunar module.

The astronauts were able to transfer to the lunar module and started working on building a CO_2 scrubber from existing materials. Mission Control engineers rapidly began working on the problem as well. Together, they were able to "MacGyver" or hack together a makeshift scrubber using cardboard from an onboard manual, duct tape, and a plastic bag with lithium hydroxide. It worked! Immediately, the carbon dioxide levels began to drop to an acceptable level for breathing.

In order to return to earth safely, they had more problems to solve. New complex calculations and trajectories needed to be determined which had never before been attempted. Also, they had to figure out a new way to separate the Lunar Module from the command module for reentry. To complicate things even more, they began drifting off-course and had to make corrective short rocket burns while conserving every microwatt of power. Using all the NASA resources and a total team approach, they adeptly made the proper calculations; they determined a way to disconnect the lunar module, and completed the course corrections. As a result, the astronauts of Apollo 13 were able to make a life-saving reentry and safe splashdown back on earth. [11] [12]

THE POINT

Although the Apollo 13 mission had to shift their goals from moon exploration to rescuing the crew, the change in the purpose of the mission resulted in saving the astronauts' lives. In a similar way, if we allow our faith to infuse our leadership, the goal of our leadership takes on new meaning. It is possible that God could use our leadership role for a bigger purpose. Perhaps this change in purpose could result in helping, improving, or even saving lives.

JOSHUA'S GOAL

We can learn incredibly significant principles from the leadership of Joshua and the way he led the people of Israel. We can see these principles in five key ways: his <u>cause</u> to believe in, his <u>courage</u> to lead, his <u>character</u> to honor God, his <u>conviction</u> to follow through, and the <u>covenant</u> he renews.

Chapter 3

CAUSE TO BELIEVE IN

There is something powerful about a compelling cause; a cause that calls us outside of ourselves in hopes of making a difference. Most people want a cause to believe in; something that gives them a clear purpose. Whether it is fighting for freedom, civil rights, equality, justice, education, unity, and peace, or fighting oppression, pollution, world hunger, poverty, and disease. These prominent issues rally people to action. In a similar way, Joshua is tasked with rallying his people to action.

In the first chapter of the book of Joshua, God calls him to leadership and gives Joshua the compelling cause of establishing a new homeland for the people of Israel. Because much of the land was already inhabited, Joshua had basically been asked to launch a military campaign and claim the land God had given them. Under Moses, the Israelites had successfully fled their lives of slavery in Egypt yet later underwent punishment for their disobedience by wandering in the desert for forty years. Now, it was time to conquer the Promised Land.

> *After the death of Moses the LORD's servant, the LORD spoke to Joshua son of Nun, Moses' assistant. He said, "Moses my servant is dead. Therefore, the time has come for you to lead these people, the Israelites, across the Jordan River into the land I am giving them. I promise you what I promised Moses: 'Wherever you set foot, you will be on land I have given you— from the Negev wilderness in the south to the Lebanon mountains in the north, from the Euphrates River in the east to the Mediterranean Sea in the west, including all the land of the Hittites.' No one will be able to stand against you as long as you live. For I will be with you as I was with Moses. I will not fail you or abandon you. (Joshua 1:1-5, NLT)*

It must have been a bit overwhelming and intimidating to be called to such a great task, but Joshua rose to the challenge. Generations earlier, God had first promised the land to Abraham in Genesis 15. Now hundreds of years later, Joshua had the honor of seeing God fulfill His covenant promise and provide a new homeland for the people of Israel. Joshua took up the cause, and then inspired his people and his army to take up the cause as well.

COURAGE TO LEAD

As the torch of leadership passed from Moses to Joshua, fear began to rise within Joshua. The pressure and weight of having to lead and be responsible for over a million people must have been heavy *(over 600,000 men plus women and children- Numbers 26:51)*. Not to mention, it is never easy to replace a great leader, especially one like Moses. No wonder God's words to Joshua at the outset are to "be strong and courageous."

> *Be strong and courageous, for you are the one who will lead these people to possess all the land I swore to their ancestors I would give them. Be strong and very courageous. Be careful to obey all the instructions*

Chapter 3

> *Moses gave you. Do not deviate from them, turning either to the right or to the left. Then you will be successful in everything you do. Study this Book of Instruction continually. Meditate on it day and night so you will be sure to obey everything written in it. Only then will you prosper and succeed in all you do. This is my command—be strong and courageous! Do not be afraid or discouraged. For the LORD your God is with you wherever you go. (Joshua 1:6-9, NLT)*

It takes courage to lead well. Often, good leaders have to swallow hard and face their own internal fears, summon their bravery, and take a leap of faith hoping and praying that God will help them along the way. Leadership can be scary, and fear can be paralyzing. I think that's why Joshua is one of my favorite leaders. I love how God calls him out of his fear and challenges him to be courageous. I appreciate His faith and courage to take over the leadership of the Israelites and not let his fear of failure, fear of the unknown, or any other fears get in the way of following God. Joshua took God's words to heart, courageously embraced his new role, and overcame his fear and discouragement.

In order to ensure his success, God urges Joshua to obey his commands and hold on to the Word of God. He repeats the call to be courageous and promises to be with Joshua wherever he goes as he tackles the massive and daunting task of conquering the Promised Land and ensuring the Israelites' survival.

CHARACTER TO HONOR GOD

Without strength of character, our leadership is open to corruption. Pride, ego, and arrogance can turn our leadership into a self-centered dictatorship. Greed and the love of money can turn our leadership into a destructive mad scramble for bigger profits at any cost. The lust for power and the abuse of that power can turn our leadership into a graveyard of mistreated workers and broken relationships. It is amazing how quickly a lack of character can destroy a leader's career and undermine his or her leadership effectiveness. Be warned... your character matters. Your ability to hold to high morals, ethics, virtues, and values defines your character. Here's another way to put it:

> "It takes faith to live by principles, especially when you see people close to you get ahead in life by lying, cheating, indulging, manipulating, and serving only themselves. What you don't see, however, is that breaking principles always catches up to them in the end.... Putting principles first is also the key to becoming a person of character." [13]

According to leadership experts, Stephen and Sean Covey, and their books about "The 7 Habits of Highly Effective People," they point out that our personal development and character help form our personal victory which lays the groundwork for public success. "Habits 1, 2, and 3 deal with self-mastery. We call it the 'private victory.' Habits 4, 5, and 6 deal with relationships and teamwork. We call it the 'public victory.' You've got to get your personal act together before you can be a good team player. That's why the private victory comes before the public victory. The last habit, Habit 7, is the habit of renewal. It feeds all of the other six habits." [14]

Leading well demands high character and Joshua modeled this well. Joshua had strong character rooted in a deep desire to honor God. He knew it wasn't all about him, and he knew that the people he led needed to focus their attention on the Lord and not on him. Joshua understood his purpose well, and part of that purpose was to guide the spiritual well-being of his people as well as their physical health and safety. So, right at the beginning of their conquest, Joshua gives the people a physical reminder of God's presence and power. Joshua took time for renewal by giving the people an object lesson using stones from the river to help them pause and remember the Lord.

> The people crossed the Jordan on the tenth day of the first month. Then they camped at Gilgal, just east of Jericho. It was there at Gilgal that Joshua piled up the twelve stones taken from the Jordan River. Then Joshua said to the Israelites, "In the future your children will ask, 'What do these stones mean?' Then

Chapter 3

> you can tell them, 'This is where the Israelites crossed the Jordan on dry ground.' For the LORD your God dried up the river right before your eyes, and he kept it dry until you were all across, just as he did at the Red Sea when he dried it up until we had all crossed over. He did this so all the nations of the earth might know that the LORD's hand is powerful, and so you might fear the LORD your God forever." (Joshua 4:19-24, NLT)

Joshua used these twelve stones from the river to set up a memorial to the Lord. In doing so, Joshua points to God and not his own ability. These stones served as a reminder to the people emphasizing God's miraculous power. The rocks symbolized that in this spot God showed up! In the days ahead, when you doubt; when you forget; when you wonder, look at these rocks and remember what the Lord did. Remember that the Lord is with us. Remember that the Lord cares about us. Remember to fear God and put your faith in Him. Remember. According to theologian Eugene Peterson, it's in remembering the past acts of God, that we can have hope for the future, and peace and joy in the present.[15]

CONVICTION TO FOLLOW THROUGH

Sometimes God asks us to do strange things that we don't understand at the time. For Joshua and his army, the Battle of Jericho was one of those times. I am not a military strategist, but I can tell you that this was not a normal battle strategy. Instead of attacking the city straight on or using stealth and the element of surprise, God asks them to march around the city walls of Jericho for seven days in full view of the enemy. The first battle of their campaign was an odd one, but one that would leave a lasting memory of the power of God.

> Now the gates of Jericho were tightly shut because the people were afraid of the Israelites. No one was allowed to go out or in. But the LORD said to Joshua, "I have given you Jericho, its king, and all its strong

warriors. You and your fighting men should march around the town once a day for six days. Seven priests will walk ahead of the Ark, each carrying a ram's horn. On the seventh day you are to march around the town seven times, with the priests blowing the horns. When you hear the priests give one long blast on the rams' horns, have all the people shout as loud as they can. Then the walls of the town will collapse, and the people can charge straight into the town." (Joshua 6:1-5, NLT)

Joshua obeyed the Lord's orders. It was an unconventional battle plan to say the least, but he didn't question his Commander and Chief. He could have, but he didn't. Instead, Joshua had the faith and conviction to follow through with what the Lord asked even when it did not make sense to him. He trusted God, and God's battle plan. Joshua's commitment to hold tightly to his beliefs and live out his faith in God showed the strength of his conviction.

In my study and learning about the Battle of Jericho, some scholars believe that sending the priests with horns ahead of the Ark of the Covenant and having the soldiers march around the city was an unusual tactic. It was like having the victory parade before they even fought the battle.

So Joshua called together the priests and said, "Take up the Ark of the LORD's Covenant, and assign seven priests to walk in front of it, each carrying a ram's horn." Then he gave orders to the people: "March around the town, and the armed men will lead the way in front of the Ark of the LORD." (Joshua 6:6-7, NLT)

When the people heard the sound of the rams' horns, they shouted as loud as they could. Suddenly, the walls of Jericho collapsed, and the Israelites charged straight into the town and captured it. (Joshua 6:20, NLT)

Chapter 3

This battle is nothing short of miraculous. Marching around a city, blowing horns, and shouting should not have worked, but it did. We can try to analyze and theorize about it like: Did all of the stomping and shouting cause vibrations that caused an earthquake? Who knows? The bottom line is this: God showed up and the walls of the city fell down. Joshua's conviction, the army's obedience, and the people's faith all combined to work in harmony with the Lord's plan. As a result, God gave them their first victory over the city of Jericho. Joshua's trust in God is a great example of the kind of conviction and trust that we need in order to lead well.

COVENANT TO RENEW

It is no surprise that sometime after the battle of Jericho, Joshua had the people take time to honor God. As Joshua switched gears from military commander to community leader, he built an altar on top of a mountain. He had the people of Israel participate in, what I would call, a "Covenant Renewal Ceremony." It was an extended time of worship, teaching, and instruction that renewed the foundation of their faith. Because God had established a special covenant relationship with the people of Israel through Abraham and Moses, it was up to Joshua to help the people fulfill the responsibilities and guidelines that God had given them. Being in a new land, it was especially important to remember their roots and hold fast to the Lord and Moses teachings.

> *Then Joshua built an altar to the LORD, the God of Israel, on Mount Ebal. He followed the commands that Moses the LORD's servant had written in the Book of Instruction: "Make me an altar from stones that are uncut and have not been shaped with iron tools." Then on the altar they presented burnt offerings and peace offerings to the LORD. And as the Israelites watched, Joshua copied onto the stones of the altar the instructions Moses had given them. (Josh. 8:30-32, NLT)*

Joshua then read to them all the blessings and curses Moses had written in the Book of Instruction. Every word of every command that Moses had ever given was read to the entire assembly of Israel, including the women and children and the foreigners who lived among them. (Josh. 8:34-35, NLT)

As leaders, getting everyone on the same page is a big deal, especially when leading a very large group of people. Joshua had all the tribes and families attend so that everybody would be informed and become an active participant in the faith of their community. In this way, they were all accountable to God, and there was no excuse for improper behavior, missed instructions, false teachings, or unclear expectations. More than that, they all renewed their commitment to follow God as a unified group. Keeping God central in the hearts of the people while living and fighting in a foreign land would not be easy, but it was an essential function of Joshua's leadership and ours.

THE CHANGE: Purpose + Faith

How does infusing faith into our leadership affect our purpose? Faith refocuses our purpose and the goal of our leadership in three key ways. By establishing a healthy spiritual life, private life, and community life, our faith can refocus our leadership goals.

Spiritual Life: Faith-based leadership requires that one of our primary goals is to honor God no matter what our leadership role is. Loving God is the first and greatest command, and it is one of the main purposes of our lives (Deuteronomy 6:4-5). We must seek to honor God first, over and above any company goals, team goals, family goals, or personal goals. While these other things are important, they must be secondary. When we infuse faith into our leadership, honoring the Lord with our lives and leadership becomes our greatest cause. In doing so, we open the door for God to reveal more specific causes, plans, and purposes that He has for each of us.

Private Life: Leading with strong inner character and acting with personal and moral integrity is critical to the longevity and effectiveness of our leadership. Acting and leading with professional

Chapter 3

ethics and a high level of personal morality protects our leadership and keeps us in leadership. When we compromise these things, our character suffers, and it undermines our leadership. According to leadership expert Dr. Tim Elmore, leadership is like an iceberg. *"The 10% above the water is your skill. The 90% below the water is your character. It's what's below the surface that sinks the ship."* [16] Keeping a tight rein on our public and private lives is crucial to leading well. Faith-based leadership seeks to live out biblical principles and morals in our lives, to avoid sinful behaviors, and to pursue personal accountability.

Community Life: Faith-based leadership identifies that another one of our primary goals is to love people. Loving others is the second greatest command, and it is also one of the main purposes of our lives (Matthew 22:36-40). If we are to lead well, we must care for the well-being of those under our leadership no matter what our leadership role is. Caring for those we lead is a common part of leadership, but not every company, team, or family is good at doing it. Faith-based leadership pushes us to become really good at caring about the physical needs and the spiritual needs of those we lead. The purpose of faith-based leadership is not only to lead people well, but also to help people follow God. In addition to other responsibilities, leading well means caring about the hearts, souls, and lives of others.

LEADERSHIP SPOTLIGHT: THE EFFECTS OF COVID-19

When COVID-19 hit in 2020, the world changed. In order to combat a global pandemic, companies had to change, jobs had to change, schools and churches had to change, leadership had to change, and people had to change. At the request of world leaders, companies stopped their normal production of products and started making masks and emergency supplies. Many of these companies experienced a change in purpose from making money to human survival. Pharmaceutical companies ceased normal operations and began working on vaccines. A fellow graduate from Taylor University experienced such a change at Pfizer pharmaceuticals.

> *In his role as a bioanalytical chemist at Pfizer, Dawdy is one of the scientists whose efforts led to the successful development of the world's first vaccine against Covid-19.*
>
> *Dr. Andrew Dawdy stated, "For my colleagues and me, it was an 'all hands on deck' situation where we each played a little piece. Together, we just figured out a way to do this ...with speed, but with the same quality standards that we always use. We figured out ways to do things more efficiently, ways to work more effectively together, performing tasks in a way we hadn't before just to get it all done. It involved doing a lot of things in parallel."* [17]

For many people and companies during COVID-19, their goals changed and shifted to help fight the virus. Some amazing collaboration and teamwork emerged as countries, companies, and people from multiple disciplines began working on the problem together.

Even still, life was different. People were dying. Things shut down. Quarantines went into effect and the world was afraid. Borders were closed and hospitals were overcrowded. Many aspects of life shifted to an online environment. Zoom video meetings and hand sanitizers became the norm. The goals of survival, health, and safety took precedence over and above everything else. This change in purpose was significant and costly but needed.

During this time, many leaders had to change their priorities, rethink their approach, shift their purpose, scrap things, remake things, start over, or completely redesign stuff. One thing is for sure, COVID-19 got people re-evaluating their lives.

Leading well requires that we re-evaluate our purpose from time to time and make sure that our leadership is in alignment with God's purposes. What if God wants to redesign your leadership? What if there is a divine purpose to your leadership role that you haven't considered or possibly one you've neglected? Maybe God wants to use your leadership in a new way or in a more God-honoring way.

Chapter 3

Whatever your leadership role is and whatever your leadership goals have been, I urge you to consider how your faith might cause a change in the purpose of your leadership and ultimately improve it.

FROM THE TRENCHES
WHAT DOES IT TAKE TO LEAD WELL IN YOUR LEADERSHIP CONTEXT?

"LEADING WELL TAKES CHARACTER, VISION, AND DEVELOPMENT. CHARACTER DEFINES US ABOVE ALL ELSE. CASTING THE VISION OF WHO A GROUP CAN BECOME IS ESSENTIAL. THEN DEVELOPING EVERYONE THROUGH INTENTIONAL MODELING, COACHING, AND GUIDANCE TOWARD THAT VISION" [18]

-BRENT GLOVER: WORSHIP PASTOR
SALTY CHURCH, FLAGLER BEACH, FL

PUTTING IT INTO PRACTICE:
What does a change in <u>purpose</u> mean to you?

Before you move on, think about, discuss, and apply the following questions as they relate to your leadership within your company, team, church, school, or family.

Leadership Thoughts

1. What key points stick out to you from this chapter and why?
2. How does infusing faith into your leadership affect your purpose?
3. Spiritual Life: How is your love for God reflected in your leadership?
4. Private Life: How would you describe your inner character, morals, and ethics?
5. Community Life: How do you show love to the people you lead and care for their hearts, souls, and lives?
6. How have you had to show courage in your leadership, and what might be a courageous next step to take?

CHAPTER 4
CHANGE IN VALUES:
What's Important?
Featured Leader: Jesus

I don't usually like to watch Reality TV shows, but on occasion I have seen a few episodes of "Extreme Makeover: Home Edition," "Survivor," "Fixer Upper," and other shows like them. While randomly catching an episode of "Undercover Boss," I was struck by the biblical principle of servanthood that I witnessed. I watched as the CEO and owner of the company went "undercover" as a bottom-level employee at a restaurant. Seeing him running food, bussing dirty tables, taking out the overflowing trash, washing gross dishes, and dealing with poor conditions reminded me of what Jesus did when he took up the towel of a house servant and washed the disciples' feet.

Strangely, I couldn't stop watching the show. I felt compelled to watch as another boss took up a shovel, hose, and rubber boots to spend the day cleaning disgusting animal stalls at the zoo. Cleaning up after cats and dogs is one thing, but cleaning up after elephants and rhinos is next-level stuff! The idea of the boss getting dirty and placing himself in the shoes of his employees in order to identify with them was an intriguing concept that often led to making major improvements to the company. There is an important leadership lesson that the TV show and the Bible both highlight and that is the VALUE of people.

Chapter 4

JESUS' EXAMPLE

We can learn extremely valuable leadership principles from the life of Jesus and the way he valued people. We can see these principles in key ways as He was <u>sent</u> by God, through His <u>service</u> and <u>sacrifice</u> for others, and how He provides <u>salvation</u> and <u>support</u> for His followers.

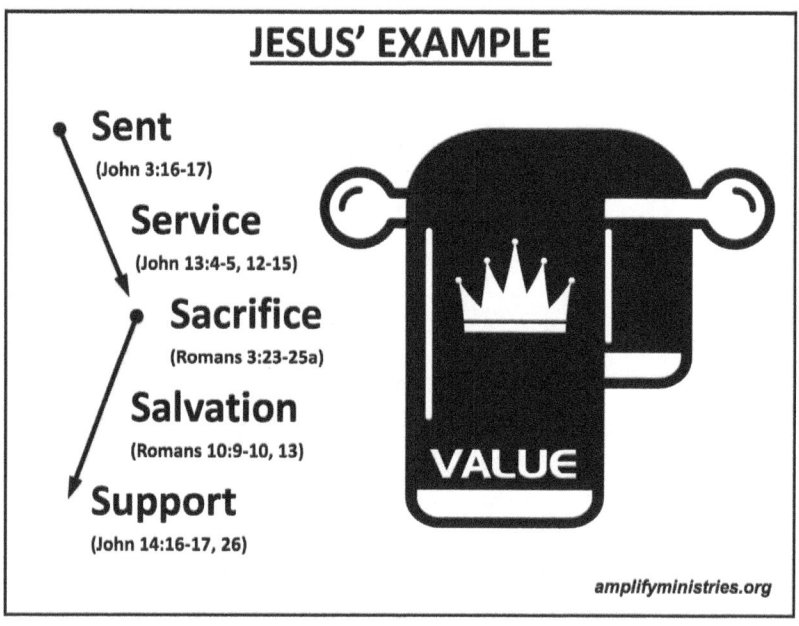

SENT BY GOD

In many ways, Jesus was the original "Undercover Boss." God sent his son to earth to be His representative. Jesus came down from His throne in heaven to live among us. He took his divine nature and wrapped himself in human flesh. "So the Word became human and made his home among us. He was full of unfailing love and faithfulness. And we have seen his glory, the glory of the Father's one and only Son" (John 1:14, NLT). Out of love for humanity, God sent Jesus on a rescue mission to restore us back into a relationship with Himself.

For God so loved the world that he gave his one and only Son, that whoever believes in him shall not perish but have eternal life. For God did not send his Son into the world to condemn the world, but to save the world through him. (John 3:16-17, NIV)

You are loved. You are loved by God. You are so loved by God that He sent Jesus as proof of His love for you. You are that important and valuable to God. You are so valuable to Him that Jesus left heaven to come to earth to communicate God's extreme love for you and for all people.

So, what does that have to do with leadership? Well, every leader needs to know deep down that he or she is loved by God. Because once you know how deep and wide God's love is for you and how valuable you are to Him, then you are free to lead and serve others. Because your core need to feel loved and important has already been satisfied, God's love frees you to be sent out to love and care for the needs of others. God sent Jesus. Now Jesus sends us.

SERVICE TO OTHERS

It is easy to be selfish. We are born that way. It is in our nature to be self-focused. You don't have to tell a child or a teenager to think about their own needs, wants, and desires. They do it naturally. However, it is quite unnatural to be others-centered and it takes a great deal of effort and training to put other people's needs ahead of our own. Serving others is a learned behavior, not an instinctual one, so it is important to have a good teacher.

Jesus is the ultimate example of servant leadership. He took off his crown, laid aside all the rights and privileges of being God, and humbly came to earth as a baby boy. Jesus flipped the idea of top-down leadership over by setting aside his rightful throne and took on the nature of a servant. He came to serve and to suffer for humanity in an amazing act of love and sacrificial leadership. Jesus is the Master teacher when it comes to putting other people's needs first.

Chapter 4

> *Don't be selfish; don't try to impress others. Be humble, thinking of others as better than yourselves. Don't look out only for your own interests, but take an interest in others, too. You must have the same attitude that Christ Jesus had. Though he was God, he did not think of equality with God as something to cling to. Instead, he gave up his divine privileges; he took the humble position of a slave and was born as a human being. When he appeared in human form, he humbled himself in obedience to God and died a criminal's death on a cross. (Philippians 2:3-8, NLT)*

When I graduated from Taylor University, I was handed my diploma in one hand and a special towel in the other. The towel had this profound inscription on it: "Christ our example of Servanthood." As we walked across the stage, they told all the graduates to take their education and go serve the world with it. The imagery was strong and the call to serve was clear. The giving of a towel had become a long-standing tradition and one that as leaders we can all take to heart.

As Jesus grew into a man and servant leader, he exchanged his crown for a towel as he washed the disciples' feet and taught them the value of serving and loving those around them.

> *So he got up from the table, took off his robe, wrapped a towel around his waist, and poured water into a basin. Then he began to wash the disciples' feet, drying them with the towel he had around him. (John 13:4-5, NLT)*

> *After washing their feet, he put on his robe again and sat down and asked, "Do you understand what I was doing? You call me 'Teacher' and 'Lord,' and you are right, because that's what I am. And since I, your Lord and Teacher, have washed your feet, you ought to wash each other's feet. I have given you an example to follow. Do as I have done to you. (John 13:12-15, NLT)*

Jesus not only gave the disciples a powerful example to follow, but he also gave all people an amazing example to live out, especially those in leadership. It is not easy to serve. Serving is messy and dirty. It takes hard work, a disciplined mind, and reliance on God's strength to do it well. Your service may go unnoticed and unappreciated, but that's the risk we take because serving others isn't about recognition it's about valuing others.

In my leadership context as a student pastor, I taught the following acronym to students as a memory tool to help them remember the value of serving others. Hopefully, it will be a helpful reminder in your leadership journey as well.

S.E.R.V.E.

- **S** erve one another in love *(Galatians 5:3)*
- **E** verywhere you go *(Acts 1:8)*
- **R** ely on God's strength *(2 Corinthians 1:9, Psalm 46:1)*
- **V** alue others more than yourself *(Philippians 2:3)*
- **E** xpress God's love with your actions *(James 2:17)*

SACRIFICE FOR OTHERS

Most of us make small sacrifices all the time. We sacrifice our time to help a friend in need. We sacrifice our money to help those less fortunate. We sacrifice our pride and ego to benefit the team. We sacrifice our popularity to do what's right. It is not difficult to give up small things for family and friends, but it is more difficult to do it for strangers. Usually, the greater the cost the more difficult it is to make the sacrifice.

Leaders are no strangers to sacrifice. According to leadership expert John Maxwell, the Law of Sacrifice is an essential part of leading well. *"The heart of good leadership is sacrifice. If you desire to become the best leader you can be, then you need to be willing to make sacrifices in order to lead well."* [19] Many leaders give until it hurts: working late, extra meetings, long hours, thankless effort, criticism, taking the heat, dealing with conflict, and constant problem-solving. Many of us often sacrifice our time, money, energy, and sleep

Chapter 4

to get the job done. However, most leaders stop short of sacrificing their lives. For Jesus, the cost of leading was high. He made the ultimate sacrifice and gave His life for His followers, for you and me, and for the world.

> *And I give myself as a holy sacrifice for them so they can be made holy by your truth. (John 17:19, NLT)*

> *... so also Christ died once for all time as a sacrifice to take away the sins of many people. He will come again, not to deal with our sins, but to bring salvation to all who are eagerly waiting for him.*
> *(Hebrews. 9:28, NLT)*

While Jesus' sacrifice is amazing, it can be hard to comprehend. Why did he do it? He did it because God the Father asked Him to do it. He did it because He was the only one who was sinless and could pay the price for our sins. He did it out of love. He did it because He cared more about us than He did about Himself. He did it despite our not being worthy of His sacrifice. He gave up Himself in order to gain something greater.

What did He give up? When Jesus died on the cross, He gave up His righteousness for our unrighteousness. He gave up His union with the Father. He temporarily gave up His throne. He swallowed His pride and embraced humility. He gave up His dignity. He lost His status. He bore the sins of the world upon His back and body as He took our punishment and our suffering. Was it terrible, awful, tragic, traumatizing, unfair, and brutal? Yes! Did He want to do it? No, but He surrendered His will to the Father and did it anyway.

Was it worth it? At the time, I think Jesus had His doubts. At the time, I am sure the disciples had their doubts. However, Jesus' resurrection from the dead puts a giant God-sized exclamation on the answer. YES! Yes, it was worth it, but at great cost. Jesus conquered sin and death in order to make a way for us to be restored to God. God the Father must have thought it was worth it or He would not have sent Jesus in the first place. From our perspective, Jesus' sacrifice was definitely worth it because we can be forgiven, have a relationship with Christ, and go to heaven. It was a risk for sure. Did we deserve it? No, and the book of Romans makes that noticeably clear.

> *For everyone has sinned; we all fall short of God's glorious standard. Yet God, with undeserved kindness, declares that we are righteous. He did this through Christ Jesus when he freed us from the penalty for our sins. For God presented Jesus as the sacrifice for sin. People are made right with God when they believe that Jesus sacrificed his life, shedding his blood... (Romans 3:23-25a, NLT)*

> *He himself is the sacrifice that atones for our sins— and not only our sins but the sins of all the world. (1 John 2:2, NLT)*

Did we deserve Jesus' sacrifice? No, but in the end, God decided you were worth it. Through His sacrifice, you, me, and the whole world benefits. If that doesn't convey the value of people, I don't know what does. Jesus sets the bar high, and as leaders, we have a lot to learn from Him.

SALVATION FOR ALL

Jesus was sent by God, served others, and sacrificed himself all for our salvation. There's no way around it. His whole mission was designed to save us all. Through Jesus' death and resurrection, He was able to provide forgiveness for all of our sins and restore us back to God the Father. This salvation is available to anyone and everyone who puts faith and trust in Him.

> *If you confess with your mouth that Jesus is Lord and believe in your heart that God raised him from the dead, you will be saved. For it is by believing in your heart that you are made right with God, and it is by confessing with your mouth that you are saved.... for*

Chapter 4

> *'Everyone who calls on the name of the LORD will be saved.' (Romans 10:9-10, 13, NLT)*

> *Christ suffered for our sins once for all time. He never sinned, but he died for sinners to bring you safely home to God. He suffered physical death, but he was raised to life in the Spirit. (1 Peter 3:18, NLT)*

Most people don't believe they need saving, and most people have not put their faith in Jesus. As leaders, it is not easy to admit we need help; that we need someone to rescue us. We are used to being strong, independent people that others turn to for help. Well, it is time to get real with yourself, to look inward, to reflect, and to evaluate the state of your soul. If you really want to lead well, you have to deal with your shortcomings, confess your mistakes, turn to God, and follow Him. Leading well requires faith.

So, I ask you in the privacy of your own mind, have you put your faith in Jesus Christ? If so, that's wonderful! You are on your way toward leading well. If not, that's ok, but it is going to be hard to put the principles of this book into practice on your own. As a friend, I urge you to keep reading, keep an open mind, and consider taking a step of faith. Respectfully, and if and when you are ready, here is a simplified way to begin your faith journey. It starts with these four words: Love, Rebellion, Sacrifice, and Faith.

- **God's LOVE:**
  He loves you *(John 3:16)*

- **Our REBELLION:**
  We all sin and make mistakes *(Romans 3:23)*

- **Jesus' SACRIFICE:**
  He died on the cross for your sins & rose again *(Romans 5:8)*

- **Our FAITH:**
  We believe and ask Him to forgive us *(1 John 1:9)*

amplifyministries.org

PRAYER OF FAITH

God, thank you for your love. Forgive me for my rebellion and sin. I accept Jesus' sacrifice on the cross as payment for my sins. I believe and put my faith in Jesus today. Amen.

Putting our faith in Jesus is at the heart of faith-based leadership. I truly believe that's where leading well begins. However, it is not a requirement for leadership. Lots of people can lead from all different backgrounds and belief systems. There are some amazing leaders in the world and in our communities from all walks of life. We can all learn about leadership from the biblical characters in this book regardless of our faith perspectives. I strongly believe that the *best* leadership and *best* types of leaders come from people whose hearts are surrendered to God.

Salvation for all. That's why Jesus came. He came to rescue us. Once we've been rescued, we can participate in His mission by helping to rescue others. Check out these words from the Bible about our salvation and redemption:

> *You have been taught the holy Scriptures from childhood, and they have given you the wisdom to*

Chapter 4

> *receive the salvation that comes by trusting in Christ Jesus. (2 Timothy 3:15, NLT)*

> *For he has rescued us from the dominion of darkness and brought us into the kingdom of the Son he loves, in whom we have redemption, the forgiveness of sins. (Colossians 1:13-14, NIV)*

SUPPORT FOR HIS FOLLOWERS

After He died on the cross, rose again, and returned to heaven, Jesus sent a representative to be with us, to help us, and to support us in our faith. He sent the Holy Spirit to guide us, to teach us, and to live within His followers. The Holy Spirit acts as a spiritual and moral conscience guiding us in how to live and act in order to please God and follow the Bible.

> *And I will ask the Father, and he will give you another Advocate, who will never leave you. He is the Holy Spirit, who leads into all truth. The world cannot receive him, because it isn't looking for him and doesn't recognize him. But you know him, because he lives with you now and later will be in you.... But when the Father sends the Advocate as my representative—that is, the Holy Spirit—he will teach you everything and will remind you of everything I have told you. (John 14:16-17, 26, NLT)*

> *But you will receive power when the Holy Spirit comes on you; and you will be my witnesses in Jerusalem, and in all Judea and Samaria, and to the ends of the earth. (Acts 1:8, NIV)*

Basically, we are not alone, and we don't have to lead alone. God wants to help us lead as we rely on Him and the power of His Spirit to inform and guide our leadership decisions. This is perhaps the biggest secret weapon of faith-based leadership: Christ in us- He works through the power of the Holy Spirit to energize and empower us to lead well. Louie Giglio calls this God's "Super" on our "Natural;" meaning that our natural lives and abilities become supernatural when we surrender them to Christ and allow God's Spirit to flow in and through us.[20]

However, relying on God's strength and the guidance of the Holy Spirit is a daily choice that faith-based leaders must choose to follow or not. Unfortunately, many great leaders still choose to rely on their own strength and human wisdom, and that usually doesn't end well for them or the people they lead.

THE CHANGE: Values + Faith

How does infusing faith into our leadership affect our values? Faith reprioritizes our values and what's important in three key ways.

First, leading well requires biblical values at its core. The value of serving, humility, sacrifice, and love are elevated, and people working together for the glory of God is more important than one person or company achieving greatness.

Second, the value of people is paramount. Jesus valued people. He challenged people. He loved people. He died for people. Leading well requires that we care about people, the needs of people, and the hearts of people. Faith-based leadership values people over profits, people over programs, and people over procedures.

Third, leadership at its base level is rooted in relationships. The relationship between a leader and his or her followers is critically important. Therefore, building healthy relationships with the people we lead, and team building, are vital to leading well because they build trust and connection. Jesus' style of leadership was profound and yet incredibly relational, dynamic, and personal. He met people on their level and adapted his methods to meet the needs of those around him. We see this in His relationship with His disciples and how He patiently loved, valued, and challenged them to become the best they could be.

Chapter 4

LEADERSHIP SPOTLIGHT: CORE VALUES @ CHICK-FIL-A

People matter, and Chick-fil-A knows it, believes it, and teaches it. If you have ever been to a Chick-fil-A restaurant, then you were probably greeted with a smile, a friendly person took your order, and sent you on your way with an enthusiastic "It's my pleasure!" Because Chick-fil-A values people at its core, people keep coming back, keep eating chicken, and the stores keep making money one satisfied customer at a time.

I worked at a Chick-fil-A restaurant for a short time during the COVID-19 pandemic to provide fast food and friendly service to essential workers and the community. It was a crazy time of mask wearing and even longer drive-thru lines that wrapped around the building, but Chick-fil-A's values never wavered. During my training, they repeatedly focused on four core values. "The key to Chick-fil-A's customer service training is what they call the 'Core 4.'" [21]

- Create Eye Contact
- Share a Smile
- Speak Enthusiastically
- Stay Connected [22]

We had to memorize these core values and put them into practice with each customer encounter, and they worked. Eye contact makes people feel seen and understood, smiling helps create a positive mood, enthusiasm is contagious and lifts the spirits, and connecting with people and being relational goes a long way. As a result, customers at Chick-fil-A often feel more cared about and have a better dining experience than other quick service restaurants.

For Chick-fil-A, it wasn't just training, it was about doing business differently. Chick-fil-A serves as a notable example of a company driven by biblical values who is still wildly successful as a productive business. From its unique vision and mission to not being open on Sundays, to its excellent customer service and tasty chicken, they have done a great job infusing faith into their leadership. Chick-fil-A shows us how a change in values can transform the way we lead.

> ## FROM THE TRENCHES
> ### What does it take to lead well in your leadership context?
>
> "To lead well we must first give our team the tools and proper training to do the job. Explain the why and show them how to do it. Get to know your team. Listen. Be available; be involved; be fair; be firm; be positive; and be supportive." [23]
>
> -Tim Sanchez
> CEO at Chick-fil-A, Palm Coast, FL

Chapter 4

PUTTING IT INTO PRACTICE:
What does a change in <u>values</u> mean to you?

Before you move on, think about, discuss, and apply the following questions as they relate to your leadership within your company, team, church, school, or family.

Leadership Thoughts

1. What key points stick out to you from this chapter and why?
2. How is Jesus' value system and leadership different from traditional models?
3. What biblical values lie at the core of your leadership or need to be at the core?
4. How can you build healthy relationships with the people and teams you lead and show them how valuable they are?
5. What does it look like to serve well and make sacrifices in your leadership context?
6. If you have put your faith in Jesus, how has He changed your leadership? If you have not, what would it take for you to consider putting your faith in Jesus?

CHAPTER 5
CHANGE IN STRATEGY:
What's the Plan?
Featured Leader: Nehemiah

It was soccer season, and I was coaching the Taylor University women's intramural team from Bergwall Hall. It was my second year coaching the girls of our sister dorm. My friend and I coached together and were excited because our team got to play in the Women's Intramural Soccer Championship. Like many colleges, intramural sports at Taylor University were very competitive because many quality athletes and top players would participate. Often, the best teams were upperclassmen who lived off campus and stacked their teams with talent. Everyone wanted to beat those teams, but rarely could they pull it off and take home the coveted championship T-shirt.

As the championship match between Bergwall and the off-campus women's team kicked off, my co-coach and I quickly realized our team was in trouble. The other team was very talented and well-rounded. They dominated ball control and played on our side of the field for most of the first half. They had several shots on our goal that we defended, but it was only a matter of time before they scored. Each time our offense started to make headway into their territory, the ball would get stolen, or our players would be double-teamed. We could hardly get close enough to take a shot. Our team was frustrated, and clearly the off-campus girls were the better team.

Chapter 5

The score was 0-0 at halftime, and our team had a decision to make. We needed a new strategy. My co-coach and I talked and pulled the girls together. We said something along these lines: "Ladies, we are getting beat, and we need a new plan of attack. This is your team, so you have a decision to make. Do you want to keep playing for fun, rotating players in, and sharing playing time, or do you want to win?" The girls thought it over, swallowed their egos, and decided to play to win.

After studying the off-campus team in the first half, they had one weakness—the goalie. She was an average player but not the best goalkeeper. The problem was that our forwards couldn't get close enough to shoot because the rest of the team was so good. Now, here's the crazy part. We told our team to stop playing offense! We brought everyone back on defense and told the girls that if they got the ball to mid-field to clear the ball hard into the other team's territory and run back on defense again. "Coach... no offense?" "That's right. Everyone plays defense in the second half."

We started the second half with all of our best players in and kept them in except for a short breather here and there. With only half the field to cover, our girls saved their energy and were able to kick the ball out of bounds or clear it into our opponent's territory. It significantly reduced their shots on our goal and frustrated the other team. It was strange to watch our players kick the ball away at mid-field, but very effective. As our opponent chased the ball down and brought it back up-field, or performed a goal kick, or did a throw-in, they were using up the clock. Regulation time ended and the score was still 0-0.

We had explained to our team during half-time that in the championship game, there is no overtime and that we were intentionally playing for a shoot-out. If we couldn't get to their goalie, then we would bring their goalie to us. It was a big risk, but our new strategy was to get their goalie one-on-one against our best shooters.

Before the shootout began, we selected our top five shooters and made one more strategic move. We took our star forward and put her in as goalie. Crazy, right? She was our backup goalie during the season, but rarely played that position except to give the starter a break. However, she was our most athletic player and was about a foot taller than our starting goalie and had a wider reach in order to block shots.

The tension was high as the shootout began. You could almost feel it in the air. As I remember it, the players were nervous as our first shooter lined up. She shot it and was blocked. We held our breath as they shot the ball and we blocked it! We made the next shot and so did they. Our next player missed and they missed too. It was neck and neck, and the stress and tension kept building. On the fourth shot, both teams blocked the ball. On the fifth shot, our player scored! The off-campus team lined up their next shooter. She took aim, ran up, kicked the ball hard, and our goalie made the save! We won the championship 1-0!

We all cheered like crazy and could hardly believe it! We beat the off-campus girls' team, and they were so mad about it. The victory felt amazing, and our girls did great. They trusted us as coaches, put the team first, and executed the change in strategy beautifully. Thankfully, our strategy paid off and it worked even though it was unusual, unconventional, and unbelievable.

THE POINT

While winning a soccer game is small in the grand scheme of things, we can learn a lot about the importance of a good strategy. Developing effective strategies is a core function of a leader, but not all strategies are worth implementing. Carefully weighing the pros and cons can be challenging and deciding what will work best is not easy. However, choosing honorable strategies and not just ones that work can be even more difficult. The art of leading well requires that we allow our faith to infuse our leadership and the strategies that we choose.

NEHEMIAH'S PROJECT

The book of Nehemiah records the amazing story of rebuilding the walls of Jerusalem. When Nehemiah heard that the holy city of his ancestors lay in ruins, he was overwhelmed with grief and felt led by God to take on the massive project of restoring the city. There are fantastic leadership principles that we can learn from Nehemiah and

Chapter 5

his strategy to rebuild Jerusalem as he prays, plans, provides, protects, and prevails.

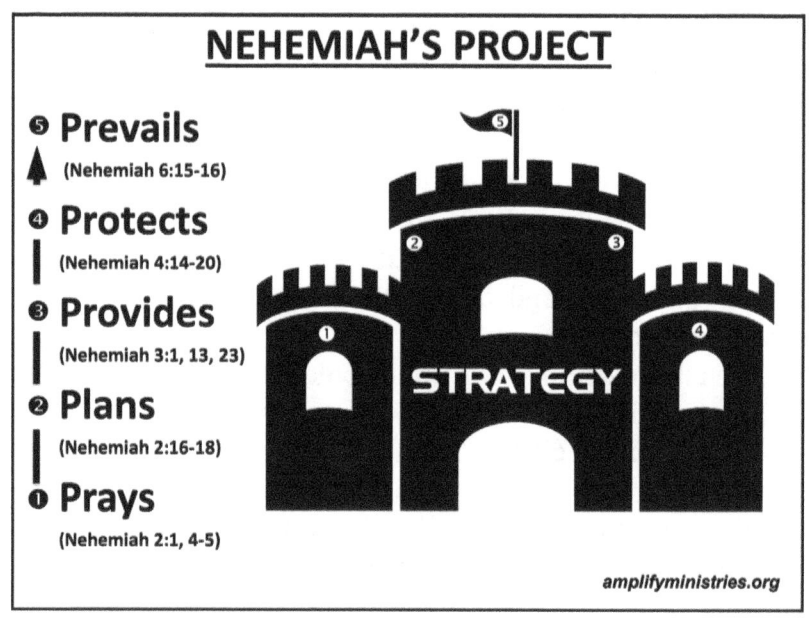

NEHEMIAH PRAYS

Struck with sadness and grief, Nehemiah began his project with prayer. He confessed the sins of his people and his own for not obeying and keeping God's commands. Nehemiah had a unique and powerful understanding that a leader's heart needed to be pure and right with God before serving. His prayer moved from purifying his heart to a deep desire to take action. He felt called to restore the city, but that meant he had to leave his current job. In those days, Nehemiah had an important position as cupbearer to the King, so he prayed for courage to face the king and to ask to leave his service temporarily and travel to Jerusalem to begin its restoration.

> *Early the following spring, in the month of Nisan, during the twentieth year of King Artaxerxes' reign, I was serving the king his wine. I had never before appeared sad in his presence…. The king asked, "Well,*

how can I help you?" With a prayer to the God of heaven, I replied, "If it please the king, and if you are pleased with me, your servant, send me to Judah to rebuild the city where my ancestors are buried." (Nehemiah 2:1, 4-5, NLT)

Prayer was an essential part of Nehemiah's leadership strategy as he continually relied on God and urged his own people to do the same. He led by example in this way and covered his project and his people in constant prayer. Throughout the whole rebuilding project, Nehemiah kept his focus by frequently asking God for help, provision, protection, and strength. Check out these notable prayers that he offers up to God:

PRAYERS OF NEHEMIAH

- **Prayer of Confession:** forgiveness and favor (1:4-11)
- **Prayer of Courage:** facing the king & request to leave (2:4)
- **Prayer of Punishment:** prays against his enemies (4:4-5)
- **Prayer of Protection:** protect our lives and the city (4:8-9)
- **Prayer of Blessing:** provide for me and bless me (5:19)
- **Prayer of Strength:** strengthen my hands to work (6:9)
- **Prayer of Justice:** remember my enemies' actions (6:14)

Nehemiah's strategy of continual prayer set him apart as a great leader because he knew that it was not all about him or his ability. Many leaders try to do things on their own strength, with their own drive, desires, and determination. However, faith-based leadership and the art of leading well starts with prayer and continues in prayer.

NEHEMIAH PLANS

Every good leader needs a plan. It is hard to be successful without one. For Nehemiah, having a well-conceived plan was a big part of what made his strategy so effective. He started with prayer, then secured favor from the king which granted him access to the king's forest to get lumber, supplies, and an armed escort. In addition,

Chapter 5

Nehemiah requested traveling papers in order to pass peacefully through several territories and began his journey to Jerusalem. Apparently, the rebuilding of Jerusalem's walls was a dangerous endeavor and something that other regions did not want. Nehemiah anticipated resistance and planned accordingly. Upon his arrival to the ruined holy city, he conducted a stealthy night recon mission and assessed the extent of the damage to the walls. He knew he was going to need help, but before he began his recruitment efforts, he wanted to quietly get a lay of the land (Nehemiah 2:11-15). With the supplies secured and recon complete, he then cast the vision to the Jewish leaders.

> *The city officials did not know I had been out there or what I was doing, for I had not yet said anything to anyone about my plans. I had not yet spoken to the Jewish leaders— the priests, the nobles, the officials, or anyone else in the administration. But now I said to them, "You know very well what trouble we are in. Jerusalem lies in ruins, and its gates have been destroyed by fire. Let us rebuild the wall of Jerusalem and end this disgrace!" Then I told them about how the gracious hand of God had been on me, and about my conversation with the king. They replied at once, "Yes, let's rebuild the wall!" So they began the good work. (Nehemiah 2:16-18, NLT)*

Nehemiah's recruiting efforts were a success, and the leaders agreed to join him in the huge undertaking. Clearly the Lord's favor was upon Nehemiah. He recruited more leaders, family groups, and tribesmen to help rebuild the walls and gates around the city. As his plan continued, he went on to provide resources and protect the workers.

NEHEMIAH PROVIDES

Nehemiah's plan included providing three more vital aspects to the project. He provided delegation, ownership, and communication.

Delegation

Nehemiah was no stranger to teamwork. He knew that the scope of the project demanded lots of help and that he would need multiple teams of people working on different areas of the walls and gates simultaneously. In order to complete the rebuilding quickly and efficiently he delegated the work to capable groups of people working together with a common goal.

> *Then Eliashib the high priest and the other priests started to rebuild at the Sheep Gate. They dedicated it and set up its doors, building the wall as far as the Tower of the Hundred, which they dedicated, and the Tower of Hananel. (Nehemiah 3:1, NLT)*

> *The Valley Gate was repaired by the people from Zanoah, led by Hanun. They set up its doors and installed its bolts and bars. They also repaired the 1,500 feet of wall to the Dung Gate. (Nehemiah 3:13, NLT)*

Ownership

One of the things I love about Nehemiah's leadership is his wisdom and insightfulness in motivating his people. Deep down he cared about them and gave them a stake in the project. He assigned people to rebuild sections of the wall behind and beside their own homes. In this way, Nehemiah gave the workers ownership and an incentive. By having them work on parts of the wall that they cared about the most, he ensured that they would do a good job, and that the quality of their work would be high. After all, no one wants the security wall behind his or her own house to be built poorly!

Chapter 5

> *After them, Benjamin and Hasshub repaired the section across from their house, and Azariah son of Maaseiah and grandson of Ananiah repaired the section across from his house. (Nehemiah 3:23, NLT)*

Communication

With so much work to be done and so many teams of people to oversee, good communication was essential. Nehemiah was good at communicating and gathered the leaders and people together for instruction, motivation, and prayer as needed (4:9-14). He also took time to listen to the needs of the workers (5:6-7). Nehemiah's ability to communicate his plan clearly to the leaders and to the workers was one of the keys to the success of his project.

Clear communication is vital. It can be the difference between success or failure. When leaders do not communicate well, teammates and co-workers get frustrated. Poor communication has been the downfall of many organizations, teams, and families. Great plans need effective communication. Leading well means taking the time to communicate clearly, efficiently, and effectively with all the people that are involved.

NEHEMIAH PROTECTS

As the rebuilding of the wall progressed, Nehemiah's opposition increased. It began with threats and distractions and culminated in surrounding regions preparing to attack them. Often when people attempt great things for God, the enemy attacks; in this case, it was quite literal. The workers became afraid and the whole project was in danger. Nehemiah had to shift from being the "Construction Project Supervisor" to being a "Military Commander." He adapted his strategy and met the needs of his workers head-on. First, he dealt with the people's physical protection. He empowered them to keep working when he posted guards, equipped all the workers with weapons, and provided a battle strategy in case they had to fight.

> *Then as I looked over the situation, I called together the nobles and the rest of the people and said to them, "Don't be afraid of the enemy! Remember the Lord, who is great and glorious, and fight for your brothers, your sons, your daughters, your wives, and your homes!".... But from then on, only half my men worked while the other half stood guard with spears, shields, bows, and coats of mail. The leaders stationed themselves behind the people of Judah who were building the wall.*
>
> *The laborers carried on their work with one hand supporting their load and one hand holding a weapon. All the builders had a sword belted to their side. The trumpeter stayed with me to sound the alarm. Then I explained to the nobles and officials and all the people, "The work is very spread out, and we are widely separated from each other along the wall. When you hear the blast of the trumpet, rush to wherever it is sounding. Then our God will fight for us!" (Nehemiah 4:14-20, NLT)*

Some leaders may have ignored the threat and pressed the people to keep working without regard for their safety. Other leaders may have completely stopped the rebuilding and prepared for war. However, Nehemiah's faith-based leadership allowed him to strike an amazing balance between rebuilding, protecting, empowering, and trusting the Lord. The heightened protection provided an increase in morale and the workers rallied to keep rebuilding the walls.

Unfortunately, a second enemy threatened the project from within, and Nehemiah had to pause to address infighting and injustice in his ranks. Nehemiah discovered that the people were upset because some of the leaders were charging interest or royalties against their own people for borrowing money, food, and supplies. Instead of dismissing it, Nehemiah listened to his people and decided to take action to provide economic protection for the people.

Chapter 5

> *When I heard their complaints, I was very angry. After thinking it over, I spoke out against these nobles and officials. I told them, "You are hurting your own relatives by charging interest when they borrow money!" Then I called a public meeting to deal with the problem. (Nehemiah 5:6-7, NLT)*

> *Then I pressed further, "What you are doing is not right! Should you not walk in the fear of our God in order to avoid being mocked by enemy nations? I myself, as well as my brothers and my workers, have been lending the people money and grain, but now let us stop this business of charging interest. You must restore their fields, vineyards, olive groves, and homes to them this very day. And repay the interest you charged when you lent them money, grain, new wine, and olive oil." They replied, "We will give back everything and demand nothing more from the people. We will do as you say." Then I called the priests and made the nobles and officials swear to do what they had promised. (Nehemiah 5:9-12, NLT)*

By addressing both the people's physical safety and economic safety, Nehemiah was able to gain the respect of his people and build unity among them. With the full attention of his people, the rebuilding of Jerusalem's walls and gates continued.

NEHEMIAH PREVAILS

In an amazing act of God with tremendous leadership, bravery, collaboration, perseverance, grit, and sheer hard work, the whole project was completed in less than two months. In record-breaking time, they had finished the walls and gates around the entire holy city. In the middle of incredible adversity, Nehemiah's faith-based leadership shone brightly as the whole community prevailed, and the surrounding nations became filled with fear.

So the wall was completed on the twenty-fifth of Elul, in fifty-two days. When all our enemies heard about this, all the surrounding nations were afraid and lost their self-confidence, because they realized that this work had been done with the help of our God. (Nehemiah 6:15-16, NIV)

Nehemiah's project to rebuild the walls and gates was just the beginning of the restoration of Jerusalem. Now the people could return to the city and begin rebuilding their homes inside the safety of Jerusalem's walls.

Nehemiah prevailed, and he did it in a way that honored God and honored the people. Sometimes leaders think that the end justifies the means, but that is not the case. In the movie "Ender's Game," the main character is a teenage boy named Ender who is trained to defend Earth from aliens by becoming a brilliant military strategist. At the end of the movie, there is this profound dialogue between Colonel Graff (Harrison Ford) and an angry Ender Wiggin:

- **Colonel Graff:** *"We won! That's all that matters!"*
- **Ender:** *"No! The way we win matters."* [24]

Ender knew the importance of not only an effective strategy but a noble one. The path to victory matters. Leading well means choosing our strategies wisely because how we get there makes a difference.

THE CHANGE: Strategy + Faith

How does infusing faith into our leadership affect how we develop strategies? Faith reforms our strategy and how we accomplish the plan in three key ways.

First, a leader's strategy to accomplish goals and execute tasks must fit with the values and purposes of the Bible. Whatever plan a leader comes up with must ultimately be accomplished in a way that does not violate Scripture. We cannot use dishonorable methods, step on people to get ahead, manipulate the truth, and bend the rules for

Chapter 5

our own advantage. Faith-based leaders are called to a higher standard of leadership. So, whether your strategy is about making money, winning the game, passing the test, raising a family, or building cars, it must be done in such a way that God is honored, people are valued, and morals are upheld because *how* we get there matters.

Second, faith-based leadership invites God into the strategy development process. Pray over your strategies, business models, game plans, and goals. Ask God to help you and your team come up with effective, beneficial, profitable, and honorable ways to accomplish your objectives. Invite other leaders and teammates to collaborate, share strategic ideas, and pray over the provision and protection of your company and employees, team and teammates, school and students, church and church members, and family and friends. In doing so, you will create a positive environment of ownership by including them and promote valuable intercommunication between people.

Third, leading well means sharing the load. Lean on your team and delegate. Don't try to do it all yourself. Delegate responsibilities to other leaders and team members. Share the vision, mission, and goals; then give them the freedom to go and do the work the best way they see fit. It may not be the exact way you would do it, but to lead leaders you must let them lead. Empower and support those around you, and you might be surprised at how people step up and get things done. Often, we can accomplish a lot more together than on our own.

LEADERSHIP SPOTLIGHT: VOLVO'S CHANGE IN STRATEGY

Finding the best strategy can be challenging. In order to improve things, we must weigh the risks and rewards and experiment with alternative solutions to achieve the desired results. Dan shares the following story about Volvo's change in their production strategy.

While working at the University of Göteburg in Sweden for a year, I had the opportunity to be involved in discussions with the head of my department on ways to improve morale and productivity at Volvo automobile factories in the area. In the 1980s, one of the problems Volvo addressed was the monotony of assembly line work and a loss of worker identity and enthusiasm.

Volvo's Plan

Many strategies were discussed, and one idea they tried was to form small units of about eight workers and have weekly meetings to get feedback on how to make the company better and increase worker morale. The result of many of these meetings was to allow the workers to have input that would help morale like music in the workplace, refreshments, and a stake in the value of the company. Later with improved motivation, they replaced the assembly line with small groups of workers assembling the car in one area, which improved worker motivation and productivity. This is a similar example to that of Nehemiah in developing a plan to rebuild the wall.

Volvo's Provision

As Volvo implemented its plan, employee ownership was enhanced because the workers themselves had more control over the workload and the pace. In the new system, they had all the parts needed to assemble one car as a team. In addition, the plant manager at Volvo relocated all managers from the central office to facilities close to the production process. Shop managers began learning more about assembly techniques, and production engineers were encouraged to interact with the workers.[25] This eventually led to better communication and incentives among the teams. It was reasonably successful in integrating technology and management in a learning "non-alienating" environment.[25] Nehemiah's principles of empowering the workers and giving them ownership in the project are similar to those used at Volvo.

Volvo's Protection

Another Nehemiah principle seen at Volvo was the issue of safety protection and overall concern for the workers. Just as Nehemiah had only half of the workers labor while the others protected them from the enemy, so in one of the Volvo plants there was emphasis on meeting the needs of the workers with enhanced concern for safety and addressing working conditions. To help make things better, work was spread out and the process of assembly was more flexible. Also, they implemented economic protection by providing workers with extra pay and incentives for increased productivity and taking on more specialized tasks.

Volvo's Production

Just as Nehemiah's workers prevailed and rebuilt the wall in a short time, the new strategy and planning at several Volvo plants increased productivity. They tested various strategies to determine the best plan for both auto production as well as worker satisfaction and health. As a result, the Uddevalla plant increased productivity by 50% in 1990-92, and they lowered tool and training costs by 50% for annual model changes compared to the traditional Göteburg plant.[26]

They often attributed their successes to the leadership strategy of a team management philosophy. Team members who excelled at special tasks were taught to become more proficient at tasks like personnel issues, recruitment, teaching, and planned days off. They also developed a team leader position designed to perform most of the tasks traditionally done by a factory foreman. The team leader was appointed by the team members and rotated over time.

THE POINT

While Volvo isn't necessarily a faith-based company, they certainly put into practice many of the leadership lessons that we learn from Nehemiah. While Nehemiah's faith in God fueled his leadership and made him an even more effective and productive leader, Volvo's change in strategy is a great modern-day example of developing a plan to engage, equip, and empower its people.

FROM THE TRENCHES
What does it take to lead well in your leadership context?

"It takes a lot of things: clear communication, explanations and details, predictions and estimations, critical thinking and considering all the variables, straight forward directions and quick responses, cooperation and being adaptive." [27]

-Dray Ely
Squad Leader: Online Video Gaming

Chapter 5

PUTTING IT INTO PRACTICE:
What does a change in <u>strategy</u> mean to you?

Before you move on, think about, discuss, and apply the following questions as they relate to your leadership within your company, team, church, school, or family.

Leadership Thoughts

1. What key points stick out to you from this chapter and why?
2. Does your current leadership plan and strategy honor God and fit with the values and purposes of the Bible? Explain.
3. How does infusing faith into your leadership affect how you develop strategies?
4. How can you better equip and empower people, delegate roles, and create ownership within your leadership context?
5. What are some ways you can improve team communication, cooperation, and participation?
6. Take a moment and invite God into the process. Pray over your strategies, plans, goals, co-workers, and teammates; ask God for His plan, provision, and protection.

CHAPTER 6
CHANGE IN POWER:
Who's in Charge?
Featured Leader: Abraham

When it comes to military leadership, it is essential for soldiers to follow a clear chain of command. There is no room for power struggles or questioning authority on the battlefield. It takes a high degree of discipline, trust, and loyalty to follow orders and surrender control to the commander in charge. Let's look at this adapted example from one of history's most powerful commanders and ruler of ancient Greece.

> *A story is told that Alexander and a small company of soldiers approached a strongly fortified walled city. Alexander, standing outside the walls, raised his voice and demanded to see the king. When the king arrived, Alexander insisted that the king surrender the city and its inhabitants.*
>
> *The king laughed, "Why should I surrender to you? You can't do us any harm!" But Alexander offered to give the king a demonstration. He ordered his men to line up single file and start marching. He marched them straight toward a steep cliff.*

Chapter 6

> *The townspeople gathered on the wall and watched in shocked silence as, one by one, Alexander's soldiers marched without hesitation right off the cliff to their deaths! After ten soldiers died, Alexander ordered the rest of the men to return to his side. The townspeople and the king immediately surrendered to Alexander the Great. They realized that if a few men were actually willing to die at the command of this powerful leader, then nothing could stop his eventual victory.* [28]

Alexander's soldiers followed his orders without question, even though it cost some of them their lives. Perhaps from his point of view, losing ten men was a small price to pay to conquer a city compared to an all-out battle. Although brutal, his leadership was impressive as was the commitment of his men. One thing is clear, there was no question regarding who was in charge. Alexander the Great was in command and his soldiers and enemies knew it. While it is hard to say if this story is completely true, an interesting legend, or a creative adaptation of other battles, it serves as a powerful leadership illustration about power and control.

While a military command structure works well in times of war, most of us do not have that kind of unwavering devotion of our followers in our everyday leadership roles. We might wish our employees, coworkers, coaches, teammates, church members, volunteers, kids, and family members were all that obedient to us, but often they are not. That type of leadership can be abrasive and abusive in the wrong context, and most people respond better to an invitation than a command.

We all struggle with authority on some level. Most of us prefer to be in control of our own lives and make our own choices rather than being told what to do. This is true even when it comes to our faith. Many of us struggle to trust God and surrender control of our lives to Him. We know in our hearts that God is loving, compassionate, gracious, trustworthy, all-knowing, and all-powerful, but we are fearful of letting go and having things happen in our lives that we don't want. Unfortunately, we often end up in a cosmic game of tug-of-war with God over who's in charge of our lives, and the harder we pull, the more unhappy and unsatisfied we become.

The Bible is full of regular everyday people who struggled to let go of control and allow God to lead and guide their lives. Abraham is one of those people. He starts off with a promising faith and gets bogged down with his own earthly plans.

ABRAHAM'S STRUGGLE

There are very helpful and revealing leadership principles that we can learn from the life of Abraham and the way he struggled for control. We can see these principles in key ways as he was <u>faithful</u> to follow God, as he was <u>fearful</u> of no heir, as he was <u>forceful</u> of his own plan, how he became <u>forgetful</u> of God's promises, and how he finds <u>freedom</u> in letting go.

FAITHFUL TO FOLLOW

I like going on adventures, but I usually like to know where I am going or what to expect when I get there. There can be something exciting and exhilarating about exploring the unknown, but it can also

Chapter 6

be risky, dangerous, terrifying, and stressful. At the age of 75, Abram was called by God to embark on such an adventure: to pack up his stuff and take his family, to leave his homeland, and to travel to an unknown destination with the promise of blessing. Sometimes following God can be scary, especially when we don't have all the details and are unsure of the outcome. I believe that's why they call it faith. Abram had faith and was faithful to follow God even when he didn't know where God was going to take him or what would happen when he got there.

> *The LORD had said to Abram, "Leave your native country, your relatives, and your father's family, and go to the land that I will show you. I will make you into a great nation. I will bless you and make you famous, and you will be a blessing to others. I will bless those who bless you and curse those who treat you with contempt. All the families on earth will be blessed through you." So Abram departed as the LORD had instructed, and Lot went with him. Abram was seventy-five years old when he left Haran. (Genesis 12:1-4, NLT)*

It is hard to not be in control. For most of us, it can be very unsettling especially as leaders because leaders are taught to have a plan, to be prepared, to analyze the options, to be organized, and to have things well thought out. After all, who wants to follow a leader who doesn't have a plan and hasn't thought things through? Infusing faith into our leadership is risky. Sometimes God asks us to do things that actually require faith. As leaders, it can be difficult to trust God at times and surrender control to Him and leave the results in His capable hands. When God asks us to do something, the question is will we be faithful to follow? Abram took a big leap of faith. He packed up his belongings, gathered his family, and went.

FEARFUL OF NO HEIR

As Abram was waiting on the Lord's timing, he began to get fearful. He was afraid that the blessings that the Lord promised would mean little if he had no son to pass them on to and carry on his family line. Abram questioned how he could have a long line of descendants without an heir. However, God promised Abram he would have a son of his own.

> *Some time later, the LORD spoke to Abram in a vision and said to him, "Do not be afraid, Abram, for I will protect you, and your reward will be great." But Abram replied, "O Sovereign LORD, what good are all your blessings when I don't even have a son?... You have given me no descendants of my own, so one of my servants will be my heir." Then the LORD said to him, "No, your servant will not be your heir, for you will have a son of your own who will be your heir." Then the LORD took Abram outside and said to him, "Look up into the sky and count the stars if you can. That's how many descendants you will have!" And Abram believed the LORD, and the LORD counted him as righteous because of his faith. (Genesis 15:1-6, NLT)*

At the time, Abram's faith prevailed over his fear. He trusted God to provide a son for him even though he was old. His belief and trust in the Lord proved his faith was genuine. However, there were more challenges waiting for him.

Do you ever get fearful that God won't come through? Have you ever wondered or begun to doubt if things will work out in the end? I have, and I think it's natural to be afraid. Sometimes fear keeps us from the things God has for us. Maybe we are afraid to fully trust God, afraid of making a mistake, or fearful of what might happen. As a result, we end up making decisions out of fear instead of faith. However, leading well calls us to push through and hold onto our faith despite our fears.

Chapter 6

FORCEFUL OF HIS OWN PLAN

Life is full of waiting. Sometimes waiting is inconvenient, like waiting in line at the grocery store, in a traffic jam, in line at an amusement park, or for a flight at the airport. Sometimes waiting can be hopeful, like waiting to hear if you got the job, for a college acceptance notification, for family or friends to arrive, or for test scores. At other times waiting can be brutal, like waiting at the hospital for a loved one to get out of surgery, for the pain to end, for someone to return, to be rescued, or waiting on God. Waiting tests our patience and our faith.

Do you ever get tired of waiting on God? It can be hard to wait for Him to answer your repeated prayers, to show you the way, to provide, or to come through for you. God's waiting room can be a lonely and difficult place. Abram and Sarai got tired of waiting. About ten years went by and they still did not have a son. Abram and his wife were getting older, and they were afraid that their time had run out to have children. So, they decided to make their own plan.

> *Now Sarai, Abram's wife, had borne him no children. But she had an Egyptian slave named Hagar; so she said to Abram, "The LORD has kept me from having children. Go, sleep with my slave; perhaps I can build a family through her." Abram agreed to what Sarai said. So after Abram had been living in Canaan ten years, Sarai his wife took her Egyptian slave Hagar and gave her to her husband to be his wife. He slept with Hagar, and she conceived. (Genesis 16:1-4a, NIV)*

> *So Hagar bore Abram a son, and Abram gave the name Ishmael to the son she had borne. Abram was eighty-six years old when Hagar bore him Ishmael. (Genesis 16:15-16, NIV)*

Abram and Sarai took matters into their own hands, and in doing so they made things worse. Understandably, rivalry and tension formed between Hagar and Sarai and later between their offspring. Abram tried to force things, but that is not what God intended. God intended to bless Abram and his wife with their own child, but they couldn't wait. They tried to speed things along by devising their own plan to have a son.

Unfortunately, the temptation to go off on our own is strong. It is hard to resist the urge to push things along when God seems slow to respond. Leading well requires patient endurance to wait on the Lord and His timing. However, when you are the one waiting, it is an incredibly difficult principle to live out.

FORGETFUL OF GOD'S PROMISES

Have you ever forgotten something important? Perhaps you forgot a birthday, anniversary, or password. Maybe you forgot your wallet, cell phone, or purse somewhere. People are forgetful at times, and that can be costly when it comes to our faith. Forgetting God's promises is a sure way to derail our faith. Unfortunately, forgetting who God is and what He can do is a common occurrence in the Bible. God must frequently repeat His commands and remind people of His promises.

In the waiting and in the fear, Abram forgot. He forgot God's promises and questions if he was really going to have a true heir. Granted, he had been waiting for about 24 years, but he forgot how faithful God is in keeping his promises. Abram left his homeland when he was 75, and at the age of 99, the Lord reminded him of his covenant promise.

> *When Abram was ninety-nine years old, the LORD appeared to him and said, "I am El-Shaddai—'God Almighty.' Serve me faithfully and live a blameless life. I will make a covenant with you, by which I will guarantee to give you countless descendants." At this, Abram fell face down on the ground. Then God said to him, "This is my covenant with you: I will make you the father of a multitude of nations! What's more, I am changing your name. It will no longer be Abram. Instead, you will be called Abraham, for you will be the father of many nations. I will make you extremely*

Chapter 6

fruitful. Your descendants will become many nations, and kings will be among them! (Genesis 17:1-6, NLT)

Abraham was 100 years old when Isaac was born. (Genesis 21:5, NLT)

Special moments in life deserve to be recognized, honored, and set apart. God's covenant with Abram was a significant moment. As a sign of God's covenant and future blessing, He changed Abram's name to Abraham and Sarai's name to Sarah. Their name changes served as a constant reminder of God's promise and of Abraham's special relationship with the Lord. Again, God promised Abraham that his wife would have a son. God was faithful. Indeed, a year later Isaac was born.

In order to lead well, faith-based leaders must find ways to remember God's promises and remind themselves and the people they lead that God is ever faithful. We must not forget what the Lord has done and what He has promised He will do. Remembering these things gives us hope and strength to face the unknown.

FREEDOM OF LETTING GO

It is not easy to let go. The struggle for control is powerful, and our leadership instincts don't give up control very often. We usually fight for it, and once we think we have it, we don't want to part with it. Feeling in control feels good, and feeling out-of-control is something we try very hard to avoid. Most leaders want to choose their own path and make their own destiny. However, there is a rare freedom in giving up control to God who knows all, sees all, and understands all things. What better person to hand the controls off to and let steer our lives than the one who made us, knows us, and is for us?

Abraham's struggle for control of his life was real, but he slowly learned to trust the Lord's plans. After 25 years, Abraham finally had a son, Isaac. Yay! God kept His promise, the covenant was secure, and the long journey was over, right? Not quite. After Isaac grew up a bit, the Lord asked the unthinkable... the ultimate surrender of control.

> *Some time later, God tested Abraham's faith. "Abraham!" God called. "Yes," he replied. "Here I am." "Take your son, your only son—yes, Isaac, whom you love so much—and go to the land of Moriah. Go and sacrifice him as a burnt offering on one of the mountains, which I will show you." (Genesis 22:1-2, NLT)*

Crazy! Why would God bless Abraham with a son only to take him away? Did God really want Abraham to sacrifice his son? That doesn't seem like the loving and caring God that we have come to trust and follow. Well, it was an extremely difficult test of Abraham's faith and a test of God's provision. Amazingly, Abraham obeyed. He took Isaac with him up the mountain and trusted that God would provide another way. He bound his son to the altar and was about to sacrifice Isaac when the Lord stopped him.

> *"Don't lay a hand on the boy!" the angel said. "Do not hurt him in any way, for now I know that you truly fear God. You have not withheld from me even your son, your only son." (Genesis 22:12, NLT)*

> *Abraham looked up and there in a thicket he saw a ram caught by its horns. He went over and took the ram and sacrificed it as a burnt offering instead of his son. So Abraham called that place The LORD Will Provide. And to this day it is said, "On the mountain of the LORD it will be provided." (Genesis 22:13-14, NIV)*

Abraham proved once again the depth of his faith in God. He released his grip of control and surrendered to God's power. He trusted God to provide, and God did. He told his son they would return together, and they did. He did things God's way, and he was rewarded. I don't think I would have had the kind of faith that Abraham had. I love my sons too much, and most dads would gladly sacrifice themselves before harming their kids. But that's not the

Chapter 6

point, God never intended to harm Isaac. The point is this: would Abraham be willing to give up that which he loved most to follow God?

It is hard to trust God at times. Being so dependent on Him can be a real test of faith. In these faith-building moments, we hold our breath because either God comes through for us or we're toast. Sink or swim, we decide to go all in on giving God control. I have had several key moments like that in my faith journey. During a difficult season of financial need as missionaries, I made a wood-burned plaque for my office with the inscription "Jehovah-Jireh" on it to remind our family that the Lord will provide. At the time, we took a huge leap of faith to follow Him. Day by day and month by month, he provided. Although our ministries and leadership roles as a family have shifted over time, He continues to provide.

THE CHANGE: Power + Faith

How does infusing faith into our leadership affect how we view and handle power? Faith releases control and changes our view and use of power in three key ways.

First, faith-based leadership chooses to surrender control to God and leans on His wisdom and guidance. Leading well calls us to release control to God and trust His leadership over us. As we let go, we can find freedom in our faithful service to God in our leadership roles. In surrendering, we become empowered by God to lead well as we leave the results in His hands and trust that he will provide what we need.

Second, faith-based leadership recognizes that our leadership is accountable to a higher power outside of ourselves or the organization. Ultimately, God is our boss. In addition to any human accountability, our leadership is subject to His authority. God is in charge, and we answer to Him regardless of our role or position.

Third, leading well invites us to handle power wisely. Because God is all-powerful and in control of all things, any power we have comes from Him or was given by Him and must be managed carefully. Leading well requires us to share our authority and power with others. By putting the power in the hands of the people who must execute the plan, we empower them to lead alongside us. There are very few situations more frustrating than when leaders hoard their power, won't listen, and won't release power to those under them so they can do their jobs well.

LEADERSHIP SPOTLIGHT: COMPANY CONFLICTS

Power struggles are common in today's leadership landscape. Countries, companies, politicians, leaders, teams, communities, and family members often battle for power and control. Unfortunately, the quest for power has led many people astray and has been the downfall of many leaders. In our society, there is no shortage of power struggles and power plays, and they often reveal an ugly side of leadership. Check out the following examples from our current culture.

What do these companies have in common: Facebook, Twitter, Google, Apple, Etsy, Volkswagen, and L'Oréal? They each have had significant power struggles within their company's top leadership. Some interesting research was done using *Forbes, Fortune, Business Insider, The New York Times*, and others which highlighted power struggles within these popular companies.

> *"Big businesses often involve big personalities and sometimes with that come clashes, with two or more people vying for the position of top dog... It should come as no surprise then that some of the most well-known companies in the world have been at the center of a power struggle or two."* [29]

According to the article, many of these power struggles involved internal conflict between founders, co-founders, and CEOs over control of the company, direction of the company, and money. Most involved at least one member being ousted and forced out of the company.

Recently, The Walt Disney Company has been in the news regarding trouble with its top leadership executives. Disney changed Chief Executive Officers in 2020, but the results were less than ideal.

Chapter 6

Former Disney CEO Bob Iger and new Disney CEO Bob Chapek were friends but aren't anymore.

> *"The timing of a CEO change at arguably the world's most famous entertainment company couldn't have been worse. Just weeks after Iger stepped down, Disney began closing its theme parks around the world during the initial stages of the Covid-19 quarantine."* [30]

> *"Anyone succeeding Iger, who had been Disney's CEO since 2005, was going to have a difficult time filling his shoes." (It would be challenging partly because Iger was instrumental in helping Disney acquire Pixar, Marvel, and Lucasfilm).* [30]

> *"In the months that followed, Chapek began making key decisions about Disney's future — including a dramatic reorganization of the company..."* [30]

> *"In October 2020, about eight months after he took over as CEO, Chapek announced Disney was strategically reorganizing its media and entertainment businesses. This was Disney's second major reorganization in less than three years."* [30]

As Chapek tried to streamline and unify things at Disney, Iger had a hard time letting go of the company and remained in the shadows as chairman of the board. Conflict grew between Chapek and Iger over the internal workings of the company, financial losses, and bad press. Their power struggle trickled down and created frustration and division among existing employees. As tensions grew, the new changes created additional power struggles among the division leaders over control of their areas of the company. *"Internal messages about business strategy from both men would sometimes conflict...."* [30] Potentially, these left employees wondering which CEO (the former or the current one) was in charge of Disney.

After receiving a three-year contract extension in June, Chapek was suddenly forced out and Iger returned in November 2022. *"Disney, in a shocking... announcement, said it had reappointed Iger as chief executive, effective immediately, after Iger's hand-picked successor as CEO, Bob Chapek, came under fire for his management of the entertainment giant."* [31]

THE POINT

Regardless of how people feel about Disney and their top-level management, the power struggle took a toll on the company. While Disney is well-loved for its theme parks and movies, their internal conflict highlights the leadership principle of "Who's in Charge?" and serves as a difficult reminder of the dangers of mishandling power. Clearly, there is a better way to lead.

In the end, all these well-known companies have struggled to handle their success and their leadership well. Thankfully, we can learn from their mistakes and forge a better path. A business article from Forbes says it best, *"Leadership is messy. Leadership is filled with difficult conversations, risky decisions, and thankless effort. There are unexpected trade-offs and ugly power struggles."* [32] It is not easy to lead well, but we must find a way to become better leaders because the need for good leadership cannot be overstated.

In our lives and leadership, the power struggle for control is challenging. Are we in charge or is God in charge? Whether you are a CEO, owner, executive, manager, supervisor, board member, political leader, community leader, military leader, emergency worker, team captain, coach, educator, parent, pastor, church leader, student leader, council member, or volunteer, we all have an important decision to make:

- *Will we invite God into our leadership, acknowledge His power, and release control to Him?*

We are all welcome to ignore the invitation, to lead on our own strength and power, and to seemingly keep control to ourselves, but it

Chapter 6

limits our leadership effectiveness, hinders our growth, and negatively affects those around us.

FROM THE TRENCHES

WHAT DOES IT TAKE TO LEAD WELL IN YOUR LEADERSHIP CONTEXT?

"IT TAKES A LOT: INTEGRITY, PATIENCE, A LOT OF PATIENCE. I ALWAYS WANT TO TREAT THE PEOPLE YOU WORK WITH THE WAY YOU WANT TO BE TREATED. TO LEAD WELL IT TAKES AN EXCELLENT WORK ETHIC YOURSELF AND LEADING BY EXAMPLE." [33]

-NICK GUTIERREZ
MULTI-UNIT AREA MANAGER AT MOE'S

PUTTING IT INTO PRACTICE:
What does a change in <u>power</u> mean to you?

Before you move on, think about, discuss, and apply the following questions as they relate to your leadership within your company, team, church, school, or family.

Leadership Thoughts

1. What key points stick out to you from this chapter and why?
2. What are some of the power struggles you have faced in your life and leadership?
3. How can you invite God into your leadership, acknowledge His power, and release control to Him?
4. How does infusing faith into your leadership affect how you view and handle power?
5. Why is power so dangerous, and how can you share it and manage it wisely?
6. In what ways can you relate to Abraham's difficulty in waiting on God, his fear of not being in control, or him trying to force his own plan?

CHAPTER 7
CHANGE IN PERSPECTIVE:
What Matters Most?
Featured Leader: Joseph

We all have different perspectives, and we each have a unique viewpoint and vantage point through which we see the world. Sometimes our perspective can be completely zoomed in on our own lives and circumstances. At other times we can zoom out and see the bigger picture and perceive a broader scope of life's meaning, purposes, and connections. Overall, it can be a challenge to find the right perspective, and a change in perspective can make all the difference.

As a scientist, my father spent a lot of time in the lab looking at cells through a microscope, but he also enjoyed astronomy and looking at the stars through a telescope. Dan shares the following illustration about the differences between the microscope and the telescope and how each one gives us a unique perspective.

We often hear the term "perspective" as it is applied to art. For instance, when looking at a painting with a road starting in the foreground and disappearing in the background, the road gets smaller in width giving the perspective of distance. Maybe you have seen a picture of a complex array of colors, lines, and shapes, and your challenge was to try and find the hidden picture. It can be hard to find until you gain a new perspective.

Another familiar example is watching a football game from different viewpoints: from the stands, from the press box, from the

Chapter 7

field, or from the Goodyear blimp. They all provide different but real perspectives. Basically, perspective is a particular way of regarding something or a certain attitude toward something: a point of view.

These are all things that can normally be seen, but now let's concentrate on the idea of different perspectives related to things that we cannot easily see. For instance, the invention of the microscope dates to the late 16th century. The development of the first microscope is generally credited to the Janssen family who were Dutch eyeglass makers. However, the person we often hear about who utilized the single-lens microscope to identify bacteria was another Dutch scientist, van Leeuwenhoek.[34]

The invention of the microscope totally changed our perspective of cell biology, medicine, and disease. Through the microscope's enhanced resolution, contrast, and magnification it became possible to observe small organisms like bacteria and viruses as well as cell structures and complex biological systems.[34] Today, we have even more powerful electron microscopes capable of magnifying objects 10 million times. More recently, using advanced technology atomic microscopes, we can see a strand of DNA and even individual atoms! The ability to see extremely small things certainly gives us a new perspective.

In contrast to microscopes, telescopes help us see things very far away. Telescopes have totally changed our perspective of the universe and our position in it. In 1608, Hans Lippershey was credited with the invention of the telescope by developing a tube and lens device that could magnify objects three times. Later, Galileo improved the telescope design with magnifications of up to 20 times which helped him describe the moons of Jupiter, the rings of Saturn, the Milky Way, Venus, craters on the moon, and other celestial discoveries.[35]

Telescopes are constantly improving and changing our perspective of the solar system and planets like Venus. The radio telescope can show radar images which go below the cloud cover on Venus and can penetrate a half mile below the surface and help map the planet's terrain.[36] For the last 30 years, the Hubble space telescope has explored distant galaxies and black holes.

One of the latest telescopes that will further our perspective of the cosmos even more is the Webb space telescope. It is 100 times more powerful than the Hubble space telescope, and it uses infrared wavelengths that can penetrate through gases and clouds. One of the most recent images transmitted to Earth was a star-forming region called "The Pillars of Creation." In fact, telescopes have helped us discover new substances that we do not understand like dark energy and dark matter.[37]

Discoveries like these will change our perspective of the history of the universe and promote the discovery of things never seen or contemplated before. As new discoveries are made, it leads to new perspectives which then lead to additional discoveries that result in changing perspectives.

THE POINT

While the microscope helps us look inward and study things that are very small, the telescope helps us look outward and see things that are very far away. Both devices offer us a unique perspective that is beyond our normal vision, and each perspective can help us see life differently.

Often in life, we can lose perspective and struggle to see and understand things in the proper light. Sometimes, a fresh perspective can make a big difference. Whether from the highest mountain top or in the deepest valley, gaining the proper perspective can take a long time and be a hard thing to find. Considering that, we can learn a lot from Joseph's journey and how God helped him gain perspective on his life and leadership.

JOSEPH'S JOURNEY

There are very difficult and insightful leadership principles that we can learn from the life of Joseph and his struggle to gain perspective in the midst of his pain. We can see these principles in key ways in the pit of betrayal, on his path to Egypt, in the prison of the forgotten, in his promotion by Pharaoh, and in the preservation of the people.

Chapter 7

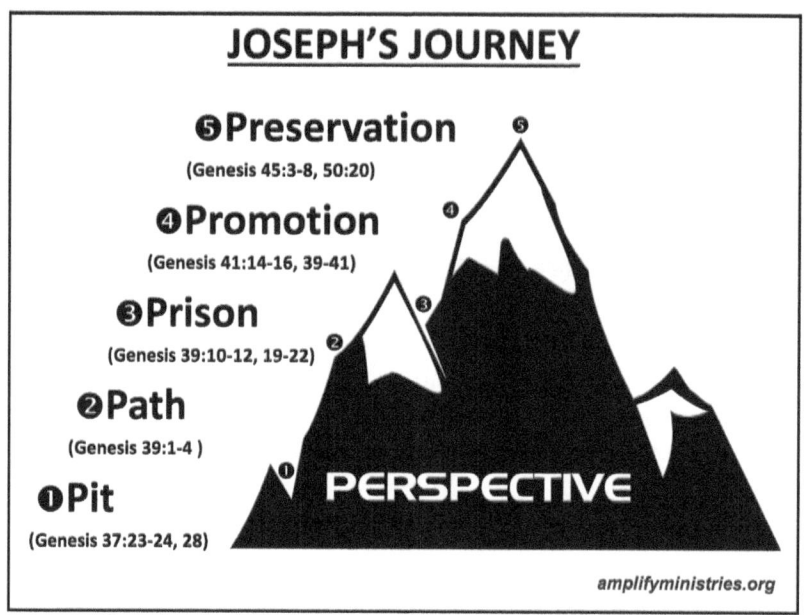

PIT OF BETRAYAL

Joseph didn't have an easy life. His journey was riddled with ups and downs, blessings and betrayal, success and slavery, joy and jail time, prosperity and pain. He had a difficult path to leadership, and it took nearly his whole life for him to gain any real perspective about what God was doing.

Initially, things started okay. Joseph came from a large family with a rich heritage. However, there was a fair amount of competition with ten older brothers. Being the eleventh son wasn't much of a birthright, but as the youngest and the firstborn of Jacob's second wife, Rachel, he quickly became his father's favorite. As a sign of favor, Joseph was given a special, ornate robe from his dad. In addition to his father's blessings, he also seemed to have the favor of God.

God had blessed Joseph with several dreams and the special ability to understand them. He shared the dreams and their meaning with his family and revealed that he would rise and rule over them, and they would all bow down to him. As you can imagine, his brothers could hardly bear the thought of it. While the dreams and their meaning were from God, you almost get the sense that Joseph was taunting his older brothers. Between their dad's favoritism and

Joseph's dreams, his brothers began to hate him. Jealousy and anger crept in, and many of their hearts turned dark. Joseph's brothers began to plot against him and planned to kill him. So, at the age of seventeen, Joseph found himself at the bottom of a pit.

> *So when Joseph arrived, his brothers ripped off the beautiful robe he was wearing. Then they grabbed him and threw him into the cistern. Now the cistern was empty; there was no water in it.... So when the Ishmaelites, who were Midianite traders, came by, Joseph's brothers pulled him out of the cistern and sold him to them for twenty pieces of silver. And the traders took him to Egypt. (Genesis 37:23-24, 28, NLT)*

Betrayed by his brothers and nearly left for dead, Joseph was sold into slavery and exiled to another country by his own blood. Joseph's journey took a major turn for the worse. Can you imagine what the scene might have been like? The brothers plotted in their hearts; they positioned themselves. They grabbed Joseph; he struggled. The look in their eyes turned dark as they ganged up on him and forced him into the empty well. He fought for his life, but there were too many of them. He fell to the bottom. Perhaps he tried to climb out, but it was of no use.

One thing was for sure: his heart must have been crushed to be betrayed by a group of his brothers all at once. How could his own family do this to him? Devastation. Sorrow. Pain. Hurt. Confusion. Darkness. For a moment there was a glimmer of hope when they pulled him out of the pit, only to be replaced with more darkness as he was sold into slavery. More betrayal. More pain. Loneliness. Grief. Loss. Anger. Abandonment and fear washed over him as he was separated from his family. Joseph's life completely shifted, as he became a teenage slave in a foreign land.

Betrayal cuts deep and the pain can linger a long time making it difficult to move forward. It can be a devastating and paralyzing experience that leaves us raw and full of questions. Why did this happen to me? Does God care about me? What's going to happen?

Chapter 7

Eventually, Joseph would have to deal with his brothers' betrayal, but for now, Joseph held on to his faith and survived. What do we do when we find ourselves in the pit of betrayal? Hopefully, we do what Joseph did; we hold on to our faith, hold on to our God, and survive. Sometimes, that's all we can do.

In times like these, leading well means leading yourself to the feet of God. It means fighting fear, anger, and bitterness with faith. It means laying it all down at the foot of the cross. It means holding on to God in the middle of the raging storm. Or we can just lay in bed and cry. Or we can scream at the sky and beat our chests in agony. Or we can drown our sorrows in a bucket of chocolate ice cream. Go ahead and express the emotion, but then release it before it devours you. It is not easy to fight the urge for revenge or the urge to give up, but we must. Leading yourself well in times of suffering means gripping your faith and taking it all to God, day by day. We must fight for ourselves so we can rise again.

PATH TO EGYPT

Reeling from the pain of his brother's betrayal and plagued with questions, Joseph was dragged off to Egypt. He was sold to the captain of Pharaoh's guard and was made a house servant. Despite being a slave and being exiled from his family, Joseph made the best of a bad situation. Amazingly, he worked hard, relied on the Lord, and quickly gained the favor of his master.

> *When Joseph was taken to Egypt by the Ishmaelite traders, he was purchased by Potiphar, an Egyptian officer. Potiphar was captain of the guard for Pharaoh, the king of Egypt. The LORD was with Joseph, so he succeeded in everything he did as he served in the home of his Egyptian master. Potiphar noticed this and realized that the LORD was with Joseph, giving him success in everything he did. This pleased Potiphar, so he soon made Joseph his personal attendant. He put him in charge of his entire*

household and everything he owned. (Genesis 39:1-4, NLT)

Joseph's perseverance and resilience were remarkable. It was very rare that a slave would earn the degree of trust and respect necessary to be placed in charge of his master's whole house. In an unusual turn of events, Joseph was rewarded with a leadership position. Clearly the Lord blessed him and helped him succeed even in some of his darkest times. Joseph's ability to keep moving forward, to press on, and to work hard despite his circumstances was a testimony to his faith. Joseph's journey is a good reminder that when we hold on to our faith and work hard for the Lord, opportunities may arise as people notice the difference our faith makes in our leadership.

PRISON OF THE FORGOTTEN

As time went on, Joseph caught the attention of Potiphar's wife. She found him attractive and tried many times to seduce him into sleeping with her. Joseph knew better than to romance his master's wife. He turned down her advances and kept his distance. Despite his honorable character, Joseph was falsely accused of taking advantage of Potiphar's wife. In her scorn, she framed him and lied about what happened. As a result, Joseph went to jail for a crime he did not commit.

> *She kept putting pressure on Joseph day after day, but he refused to sleep with her, and he kept out of her way as much as possible. One day, however, no one else was around when he went in to do his work. She came and grabbed him by his cloak, demanding, "Come on, sleep with me!" Joseph tore himself away, but he left his cloak in her hand as he ran from the house. (Genesis 39:10-12, NLT)*
>
> *Potiphar was furious when he heard his wife's story about how Joseph had treated her. So he took Joseph and threw him into the prison where the king's*

Chapter 7

prisoners were held, and there he remained. (Genesis 39:19-20, NLT)

Falsely accused. Falsely imprisoned. Joseph lost his position, and his life took another downturn. Betrayed again, he was left in prison for years and was eventually forgotten. Just when it seemed his life and situation were improving, it all fell apart again. The injustice and unfairness of his circumstances must have weighed heavy on his heart and mind.

It is incredible that after all this, Joseph earned the favor and trust of the prison warden. Joseph's faith, noble conduct, and resilience were rewarded again as he was placed in charge of the other prisoners. Even in jail, Joseph found himself in a leadership role. Again, the Lord was with him in exile, in slavery, and now in prison.

But the LORD was with Joseph in the prison and showed him his faithful love. And the LORD made Joseph a favorite with the prison warden. Before long, the warden put Joseph in charge of all the other prisoners and over everything that happened in the prison. (Genesis 39:21-22, NLT)

If Joseph took inventory of his life at this point, he would have very little perspective on what God was doing and why. His limited view from the cistern floor, from the bondage of slavery, or through the prison bars would make it incredibly difficult to understand God's will and purpose for his life. Joseph's journey reminds us that leading well requires no small amount of perseverance and faith, especially in the absence of perspective. Thankfully, this was not the end of his journey.

PROMOTION BY PHARAOH

Years went by, and the Pharaoh of Egypt began having some disturbing dreams that his advisors could not interpret or understand. The chief cupbearer who brought wine to Pharaoh was a former inmate in the prison, and he remembered Joseph and his ability to interpret dreams. Upon hearing about him, Pharaoh summoned Joseph from jail.

> *Pharaoh sent for Joseph at once, and he was quickly brought from the prison. After he shaved and changed his clothes, he went in and stood before Pharaoh. Then Pharaoh said to Joseph, "I had a dream last night, and no one here can tell me what it means. But I have heard that when you hear about a dream you can interpret it." "It is beyond my power to do this," Joseph replied. "But God can tell you what it means and set you at ease." (Genesis 41:14-16, NLT)*

Joseph listened to Pharaoh's disturbing dreams and interpreted them to mean that seven years of plenty were coming followed by seven years of famine in the land. Pharaoh was impressed with Joseph and his wisdom from God. The King of Egypt realized that there was no one better than Joseph to provide leadership over this threat to the whole nation.

Finally, after all the challenges, pain, and heartache, Joseph was lifted up in honor and promoted. At the age of 30, he became second in command of all of Egypt. It was in this moment that he got a glimpse of perspective and began to see his purpose.

> *Then Pharaoh said to Joseph, "Since God has revealed the meaning of the dreams to you, clearly no one else is as intelligent or wise as you are. You will be in charge of my court, and all my people will take orders from you. Only I, sitting on my throne, will have a rank higher than yours." Pharaoh said to Joseph, "I hereby put you in charge of the entire land of Egypt." (Genesis 41:39-41, NLT)*

Joseph's promotion from the pit and prison to Pharaoh's palace was quite a jump in status. Joseph literally went from rags to riches overnight. More importantly, Joseph began to see why God had him sent to Egypt and started to see the bigger picture that had been

Chapter 7

eluding him for so long. As Joseph gained some clarity, he was able to fulfill God's intended purpose for his life and embraced his new leadership position.

Joseph lacked perspective for a long time, but he continued to rely on God's ability to see all things. Leading well challenges us to be faithful in the small things regardless of our leadership position or vantage point and trust that God sees the big picture even when we can't.

PRESERVATION OF THE PEOPLE

As the seven years of plenty began, Joseph put a plan into action to collect and store grain for the coming famine. It was a massive undertaking, but he systematically had his workers collect a fifth of the harvest over seven years and stored it in cities for redistribution to the people later.

The famine struck hard and severely crippled the surrounding regions with starvation and death. Joseph's relief efforts in Egypt became the central hub for foreign aid to the entire population, including Canaan where his family lived.

During the famine, Joseph's father sent his brothers to Egypt to buy food. Upon their arrival, the brothers came face to face with Joseph and bowed down before him but did not recognize him. Joseph realized who they were right away, but kept his identity hidden to test them. He had one brother imprisoned as collateral, provided provisions for the rest, and demanded that they go home and return with their youngest brother to prove their loyalty. The brothers did as Joseph commanded, reported back to their father, and returned with Benjamin the youngest.

After over twenty years, Joseph was reunited with his brothers. In a powerful and emotional moment, he invited them into the palace and revealed his true identity to them.

> *"I am Joseph!" he said to his brothers. "Is my father still alive?" But his brothers were speechless! They were stunned to realize that Joseph was standing there in front of them. "Please, come closer," he said to*

them. So they came closer. And he said again, "I am Joseph, your brother, whom you sold into slavery in Egypt. But don't be upset, and don't be angry with yourselves for selling me to this place. It was God who sent me here ahead of you to preserve your lives.

This famine that has ravaged the land for two years will last five more years, and there will be neither plowing nor harvesting. God has sent me ahead of you to keep you and your families alive and to preserve many survivors. So it was God who sent me here, not you! And he is the one who made me an adviser to Pharaoh—the manager of his entire palace and the governor of all Egypt. (Genesis 45:3-8, NLT)

<u>*You intended to harm me, but God intended it all for good.*</u> *He brought me to this position so I could save the lives of many people. (Genesis 50:20, NLT, emphasis added)*

Finally, Joseph gained perspective. After all he had been through, he could see that God had a plan to use his life to help preserve the lives of all the people, including his own family. The dreams he had as a teenager finally came true. God's purpose in Joseph's suffering became clear to him as he saw the hand of God working to take what was meant for evil and use it for good. Joseph held on to what was most important: his faith. It was his faith in God that sustained him through all his troubles and allowed him to have victory over the dark times, victory over his brothers' betrayal, victory in forgiving them, and victory in becoming the leader he was meant to be.

We often don't understand why God allows pain, suffering, tragedies, and difficulties to happen. In addition, we often lack perspective and understanding of God's purposes for the hardships in our lives. However, how we face and handle adversity is a vital aspect of our leadership. Will we rise to meet the challenge? Will we overcome it? How will we handle defeat? Will we hold onto our values, beliefs, and faith even when everything is stacked against us? Or will we lose sight of what's important, allow our pain to distort our view of God, withdraw into ourselves, and sink into the darkness?

Faith-based leadership beckons us to hold on to what's important, to hold on to hope, to hold on to Jesus, and to hold on to our faith in a God who relentlessly pursues us and loves us. This type of leadership is rare and extremely valuable. It is refined in the fire. It rises from the ashes. It resists the urge to give up and the temptation to believe that God has given up. It trusts that even though we may not see it or understand it, God has a plan and that he is an expert at redeeming what was lost.

THE CHANGE: Perspective + Faith

How does infusing faith into our leadership affect our perspective and the lens through which we view things? Faith renews our perspective and what's important in three key ways.

First, faith-based leadership seeks to hold on to what matters most, and what matters most is that we hold on to our faith, no matter what. Joseph weathered the storms of life by holding onto his faith and so must we. Our faith is foundational to our leadership, and it is vital for gaining any true and lasting perspective.

Second, Joseph's journey helps give us perspective on how we view hardship. Faith-based leaders trust that God is present and at work even in our darkest times, deepest pain, and hardest difficulties. Joseph's hardships help bring some dignity to our own suffering in that God was with him in it and used his experiences to ultimately help many people. Faith-based leaders allow their faith to shine through their difficulties and trust that God will use their hardship for good in the end.

Third, the faith-based leader looks to see the big picture and tries to view things from God's perspective. While our perspective may be limited, our faith can enable us to consider things from a divine point of view. In doing so, we can try to step back from our circumstances and allow for the possibility that God has a plan beyond our understanding. A faith-based perspective can help us understand that God may be trying to accomplish something far more than we anticipated or something much bigger than what we can see. In the end, leading well invites us to ask God to give us a renewed sense of perspective about our lives and our leadership. As we seek Him through prayer and reading His word, our thoughts and perspectives can be refreshed.

LEADERSHIP SPOTLIGHT: ABRAHAM LINCOLN

Often, when we accept a leadership role, we don't always know what lies ahead. Sometimes we find ourselves in a position to change things in a way that we did not expect. At just the right time, our leadership can be used to influence others and make positive changes that really make a difference. Dan shares the following spotlight example about the leadership journey of Abraham Lincoln and how a change in his perspective impacted the whole country.

Many of us are familiar with Abraham Lincoln as the sixteenth President of the United States from 1861-1865. However, what is not often known is the difficult pathway he traveled to get there. Lincoln scholar Harry V. Jaffe wrote: *"No political leader in all human history began his office in the midst of more profound difficulties nor a situation in which his leadership depended upon such contrary imperatives."* [38] Let's look at some of the challenges he faced.

Pit of Adversity

To begin, Lincoln ran for Illinois state legislature in 1832 and lost. He was defeated as state Speaker of the House in 1838. He lost the nomination for Congress in 1843. He was rejected in his run for state Land Officer in 1849. In 1854 he was defeated for the U.S. Senate. He lost the nomination for U.S. Vice President in 1856 and was again defeated for a U.S. Senate seat in 1858. [39] At this point in his journey, Lincoln had lost many political races and faced a lot of adversity. He may have even wondered if he would ever make it as a political leader. In a letter to Henry Asbury, Lincoln expressed his determination: *"The fight must go on. The cause of civil liberty must*

Chapter 7

not be surrendered at the end of one, or even one hundred defeats... - November 19, 1858." [40]

Path to Presidency

Lincoln's path to the presidency was not easy and he experienced a lot of rejection along the way. Lincoln was determined not to give up, and he kept going. He continued to apply for positions and run for office. Finally, with unbelievable perseverance, he won the Presidency in 1860. In a letter to William Seward, President Lincoln wrote: *"I expect to maintain this contest until successful, or till I die, or am conquered, or my term expires, or Congress or the country forsakes me... -June 28, 1862."* [40]

Persistent Faith

How was Lincoln able to keep persevering through all the challenges that were before him? One of the reasons he was able to move from failure to success can be attributed to his faith in God. One of Lincoln's quotes gives us insight into his persistent faith: *"But it has pleased Almighty God to place me in my present position, and, looking up to Him for wisdom and divine guidance, I must work out my destiny as best I can."* [41] Lincoln had a reverence for the Lord and relied on God for guidance.

Perspective on Slavery

One of the biggest challenges that Lincoln faced during his presidency was the issue of slavery. He was against slavery. However, during his first year as President, with various factions pulling him in opposite directions, he followed a middle course between the slaveholding Southerners and their opponents in the North. In the span of a few years, as the Civil War consumed his presidency, Lincoln's views on slavery shifted drastically. His perspective on slavery changed, and he even began to promote full equality for Blacks.[42] [43] Lincoln played an important role in freeing the slaves via the Emancipation Proclamation and banning slavery with the 13th Amendment.

Preserving the Future

Even though his presidency and his life were cut short when he was assassinated in 1865. Many of his ideals, values, and perspectives lived on. Lincoln's leadership helped pave the way for future generations of Americans to live in freedom. Some of the important leadership qualities of Lincoln were the importance he placed on people, looking to God for guidance, using rational arguments and persuasion rather than mandatory orders, and using reason and conscience to guide outcomes.[44]

THE POINT

Abraham Lincoln lived out many of the leadership principles from Joseph's life. They both persevered through great adversity and used their position and influence to make a huge difference in the lives of the people around them. Neither man knew beforehand how God would use them to change the course of history, yet they embraced their leadership roles well and leaned on God for guidance and perspective.

FROM THE TRENCHES

WHAT DOES IT TAKE TO LEAD WELL IN YOUR LEADERSHIP CONTEXT?

"COME PREPARED! HOWEVER, ALWAYS BE WILLING TO SHIFT GEARS DEPENDING ON THE MOOD OF THE CLASS AND HOW THE STUDENTS ARE RESPONDING TO THE CONTENT. LOVE EACH STUDENT, GIVE LOTS OF ENCOURAGEMENT, TEACH WITH CONFIDENCE, PROVIDE CLEAR BOUNDARIES, LAUGH TOGETHER, AND BE YOURSELF."

-TINA ELY
PRESCHOOL TEACHER [45]

Chapter 7

PUTTING IT INTO PRACTICE:
What does a change in <u>perspective</u> mean to you?

Before you move on, think about, discuss, and apply the following questions as they relate to your leadership within your company, team, church, school, or family.

Leadership Thoughts

1. What key points stick out to you from this chapter and why?
2. What are some experiences in your life that have given you perspective?
3. How has God been present and at work even in your darkest times, deepest pain, and hardest difficulties?
4. How does infusing faith into your leadership affect your perspective on things?
5. In what ways can you relate to Joseph's journey of being in the pit or prison, of not having perspective, of struggling to forgive, or of finding victory?
6. Pause for a moment and ask God to give you a renewed sense of perspective about your life, your circumstances, and your leadership.

CHAPTER 8
CHANGE IN OUTCOMES:
How Do You Succeed?
Featured Leader: Paul

Do you like to cook? My mom, Linda, is known for her great cooking. She makes the best homemade applesauce! It's basically like eating warm cinnamon apple pie without the crust. What makes mom's applesauce so good? She's not telling! While her secret recipe and the secret ratio of ingredients remain a mystery, "grandma's applesauce" remains the top requested food item at family gatherings. In fact, my sons love it so much they have had it sent to their friends and have frozen extra containers of it to save for later. How about you? Does your family have a secret sauce, secret ingredient, or special recipe that people crave and rave about?

Secret recipes are one thing, but what's the secret to success? More specifically, what does it take to succeed as an athlete in the face of difficult obstacles? Many Olympic athletes have overcome tremendous odds to rise up, compete for their country, and win a medal. Shaun White is a U.S. Olympic gold medalist and X-Games snowboarding champion who has faced his share of adversity.

With his iconic red hair and big air, Shaun White has become one the most well-known and successful snowboarders in the world, but it hasn't been an easy road. He was born with a congenital heart defect and underwent multiple surgeries as a child. He overcame the odds and began skateboarding at age 5 and became a professional snowboarder at age 13.[46] Shaun turned pro in skateboarding at age 17 and went on to win his first Olympic gold medal for snowboarding at age 19.[47] He is a tough competitor and a snowboarding "beast" in the halfpipe and slopestyle competitions.

However, he has faced significant obstacles along his journey. In 2014 at the Olympic games in Sochi, Shaun had a devastating snowboarding crash. He misjudged a complicated trick and landed wrong on the rim of the half-pipe. He smashed his face badly and the combined speed and height of the fall caused internal injuries as well. After crashing in the half-pipe and losing at the Sochi games, Shaun was in pain both physically and mentally. He needed time to heal, reflect, and recover.

In an interview, Shaun shared that leading up to the Sochi games something happened, "his mindset underwent a dramatic shift." [46] He lost confidence and belief in himself which in turn limited his performance.

After the pain, tears, and discouragement, he found a way to turn his negative experiences and difficult setbacks into positive motivators to improve. Shaun White shares one of his secrets to successfully overcoming adversity was developing mental toughness. He found a way to pivot his thinking and press on in the face of failure:

> *"When things go wrong, I've learned this very simple, valuable lesson of what not to do. And so when I come back, I've made new calculations and adjustments in my head of what has to happen for it to be successful.... So I'm not really starting over. I'm starting from experience. And you know that can be a very powerful thing."* [48]

Determined to mount a major comeback and overcome his fears, White returned to the Olympics in 2018 with a renewed mindset. His road to redemption was complete when he crushed the competition on his last run and won gold in the half-pipe at the PyeongChang games.[46]

Chapter 8

THE POINT

Sometimes, the right ingredient or the right mentality makes all the difference. While there may not be one big secret to leading well, there are some important ingredients. Some of those ingredients are found in Paul's leadership journey as he helps us redefine how we view outcomes and shares an important secret to his success.

PAUL'S SECRET

There are very valuable leadership principles that we can learn from the life of Paul and the way he viewed success. We can see these principles in key ways in his <u>persecution</u> of believers, as he <u>pivots</u> toward God, in his <u>provision</u> to lean on God, in his <u>perseverance</u> to press on in his faith, and in his desire to <u>pass</u> it on and hand off the leadership torch to others.

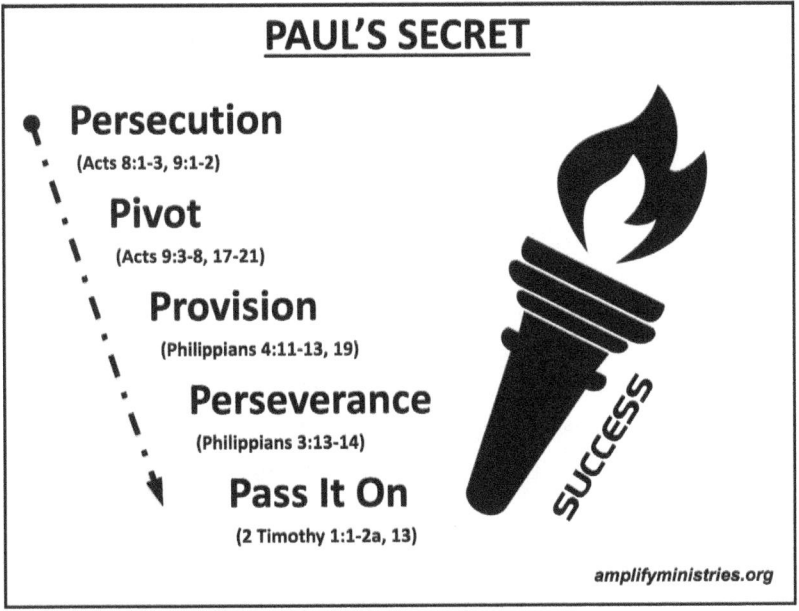

PERSECUTION OF BELIEVERS

We have a choice about how we use our leadership abilities. We can use them for good and noble causes, or we can use them for darker purposes. History is full of people with strong leadership abilities who used them for ruthless ends. Saul is one such leader. He was a Roman citizen, a devout Jew, and a Pharisee, a powerful religious leader. At the time, Saul was zealously attacking the Christian church by killing its followers or putting them in prison. He was against the teachings of Jesus and wanted to put an end to the church. Saul had great influence and was responsible for a massive outbreak of persecution against the followers of Christ. People feared him and his practices. As a result, the Christians began to scatter throughout the region.

> *Saul was one of the witnesses, and he agreed completely with the killing of Stephen. A great wave of persecution began that day, sweeping over the church in Jerusalem; and all the believers except the apostles were scattered through the regions of Judea and Samaria. (Some devout men came and buried Stephen with great mourning.) But Saul was going everywhere to destroy the church. He went from house to house, dragging out both men and women to throw them into prison. (Acts 8:1-3, NLT)*

> *Meanwhile, Saul was uttering threats with every breath and was eager to kill the Lord's followers. So he went to the high priest. He requested letters addressed to the synagogues in Damascus, asking for their cooperation in the arrest of any followers of the Way he found there. He wanted to bring them—both men and women—back to Jerusalem in chains. (Acts 9:1-2, NLT)*

Saul became notorious for his actions and the followers of Jesus grew deeply concerned for their own safety. In his zeal to protect the Jewish law and teachings, the Christian church suffered. Saul may have felt that his extreme actions were justified at the time, but his choices would come to have a profound impact on his own life. At this point, Saul had become a powerful leader, but he was not leading well.

Chapter 8

Violence and oppression are not the answer. There is a better way to lead.

PIVOT TOWARD GOD

Have you ever had a life-changing experience? Has something happened to you that was so significant that it altered the way you live? Sometimes life-changing things come from positive experiences, and sometimes they come from difficult circumstances. Most of the time they are unexpected and unpredictable. One moment, our life is heading in one direction, and then suddenly our life changes. For better or for worse, these experiences often reshape our thinking and our faith.

Saul was about to have an experience with God that would change his life, his leadership, and his faith forever. He was so good at persecuting the church that he gained the attention of Jesus himself. As he was traveling to another city to arrest more followers, Jesus appeared to him and interrupted Saul's trip in a dramatic and powerful way. Now Jesus had already died on the cross, risen from the grave, and ascended to heaven at this point (all of which Saul didn't believe). Bottom line, the Jesus he didn't believe in was now speaking with him; this was no ordinary experience! Jesus wanted Saul to stop persecuting the church and decided to make a memorable impression on him.

> *As he was approaching Damascus on this mission, a light from heaven suddenly shone down around him. He fell to the ground and heard a voice saying to him, "Saul! Saul! Why are you persecuting me?" "Who are you, lord?" Saul asked. And the voice replied, "I am Jesus, the one you are persecuting! Now get up and go into the city, and you will be told what you must do." The men with Saul stood speechless, for they heard the sound of someone's voice but saw no one! Saul picked himself up off the ground, but when he opened his eyes he was blind. So his companions led him by the hand to Damascus. (Acts 9:3-8, NLT)*

Saul's encounter with Jesus changed his life. He pivoted 180 degrees in his thinking and in his faith and changed allegiances. Basically, he realized that he was on the wrong side. He switched teams and immediately started teaching and preaching that Jesus is indeed the Son of God. Transformed by the power of Christ, Saul started using his leadership abilities to build up the church instead of trying to destroy it.

> *So Ananias went and found Saul. He laid his hands on him and said, "Brother Saul, the Lord Jesus, who appeared to you on the road, has sent me so that you might regain your sight and be filled with the Holy Spirit." Instantly something like scales fell from Saul's eyes, and he regained his sight. Then he got up and was baptized. Afterward he ate some food and regained his strength.*
>
> *Saul stayed with the believers in Damascus for a few days. And immediately he began preaching about Jesus in the synagogues, saying, "He is indeed the Son of God!" All who heard him were amazed. "Isn't this the same man who caused such devastation among Jesus' followers in Jerusalem?" they asked. "And didn't he come here to arrest them and take them in chains to the leading priests?" (Acts 9:17-21, NLT)*

Most people don't change overnight, but Saul was truly a changed man. His encounter with Jesus sparked immediate change that was followed by immediate action. He got baptized into a new faith and began preaching. It was so shocking that the Christian believers he had been persecuting had their doubts, but his life change and his change of heart were real and genuine. Saul pivoted toward God. More specifically, he turned toward Jesus, and that made all the difference.

Saul was later called Paul. He went on to become one of the greatest missionaries of all time as he spread the Word of God to much of the Palestinian region as well as Rome, Italy, Greece, and

Chapter 8

Turkey. In addition to starting many churches around the Mediterranean, Paul is well known for authoring a significant portion of the New Testament. Paul's transformation shows us the power of a changed life. It's amazing what can happen when God gets a hold of our lives and our leadership.

PROVISION TO LEAN ON

In an ironic twist, Saul the persecutor was basically recruited by Jesus and became Paul the missionary. However, the change would come at great cost as Paul would learn through his sufferings to lean on Christ for His provision. Paul went to great lengths to share the message of Christ and the love of God with people from all over the region. He was shipwrecked, put on trial, imprisoned, beaten, and suffered greatly for the cause of Christ. Through it all, he learned an amazing life lesson that would become the secret to Paul's success.

> *I am not saying this because I am in need, for I have learned to be content whatever the circumstances. I know what it is to be in need, and I know what it is to have plenty. I have learned the secret of being content in any and every situation, whether well fed or hungry, whether living in plenty or in want. <u>I can do all this through him who gives me strength</u>. (Philippians 4:11-13, NIV, emphasis added)*

> *And my God will meet all your needs according to the riches of his glory in Christ Jesus. (Philippians 4:19, NIV)*

Paul's mantra became "I can do everything through Christ." That was the secret to his success. In fact, that scripture has become a rally cry for many people of faith today. Paul believed it, and he lived it. Through thick and thin, good and bad, joy and pain, Christ was all he needed. In many ways, this redefined success for him, and it redefines success for us. It is not about profit, personal gain, recognition, or reward, it's about relying on God and being faithful to

Him. Paul realized that there was nothing he could gain in this world that could compare to knowing and following Christ. All his accolades, achievements, possessions, and prestige meant nothing in light of simply knowing and following Jesus.

> *But whatever were gains to me I now consider loss for the sake of Christ. What is more, I consider everything a loss because of the surpassing worth of knowing Christ Jesus my Lord, for whose sake I have lost all things. I consider them garbage, that I may gain Christ... (Philippians 3:7-8, NIV)*

From a guy who could brag about his status if he wanted to, this is a massive turnaround. He gave up his prominent position as a Pharisee and sacrificed his social status to follow Jesus. He went against the culture of his day and dedicated the rest of his life to sharing the life-changing message of forgive-ness and redemption through the cross of Christ. For Paul, success was going all-in on his faith in Jesus. Leading well invites us to reconsider our view of success and what it means to be successful. Being a successful person and leader is about being faithful to God and following Christ. If you do that, then you are successful no matter what the world, the metrics, or the culture says.

Faith-based leadership looks at success through the lens of faithfulness. In this regard, it doesn't matter how many people show up, how many items sell, how cool it looked, how many people liked it, how well it was trending, how many records were set, how big or small it was. What matters is... were you faithful to the task God gave you and did you honor him in it? If so, then you were successful. At this point, we give our work up to Him and leave the results in God's hands. From this point of view, everyone can be successful as a person: rich or poor, young or old, liked or disliked, teacher or student, parent or child, employer or employee, executive or truck driver, pastor or prisoner, veteran or rookie, popular or outcast.

However, being faithful to follow God doesn't instantly make you a great leader, but it does make you a successful person of faith. Leading well takes hard work, and there is always room for

Chapter 8

improvement. We should all seek to improve ourselves and our skills as we rely on God to shape and mold us into better leaders.

How we define success is an important aspect of how we lead others. In my leadership context as a student pastor, one of my favorite ways to define the key to the success of our group was through great teamwork. One of our goals was to help students work together for the cause of Christ. For us, the key to great teamwork was S.U.C.C.E.S.S.

- **S acrifice**: work hard and give above and beyond
- **U nity**: promote harmony and avoid division
- **C ooperation**: work together and follow instructions
- **C ommunication**: listen well, speak clearly, and respond often
- **E ncouragement**: support and build up your teammates
- **S elflessness**: put the team and your teammates first
- **S ignificance**: champion the cause and show value to others

In summary, through our hard work and sacrifices for one another, we promote unity and build a spirit of cooperation. With clear communication and encouragement, we inspire and motivate our team. By serving our fellow teammates, our selflessness puts the team first. Together, we find significance in a job well done.

This was an effective team-building tool for us, but it might not work for you. Because everyone's leadership context is different, leading well requires us to adapt and modify what success looks like for the people we lead. Clarify how people can be successful on your team with clear expectations and realistic goals. However, as you lead, remember the secret to Paul's success: *"For I can do everything through Christ, who gives me strength" (Philippians 4:13, NLT).*

PERSEVERANCE TO PRESS ON

As Paul left his old way of life behind and pursued his new life in Christ, he was persecuted for it. Some of the same opposition that he was responsible for creating now became an obstacle for him. His path was difficult and at times people were hostile toward him. As he chose to take the message of God into the religious, political, and philosophical arenas of Athens, Rome, Ephesus, and Corinth, Paul had to persevere. These cultural centers were important and strategic cities to go to, but they were also risky endeavors. Many people and institutions were not open to hearing about Jesus, and they often opposed Paul's message openly and secretly tried to eliminate him.

> *Not only so, but we also glory in our sufferings, because we know that suffering produces perseverance; perseverance, character; and character, hope. And hope does not put us to shame, because God's love has been poured out into our hearts through the Holy Spirit, who has been given to us. (Romans 5:3-5, NIV, emphasis added)*

> *Brothers and sisters, I do not consider myself yet to have taken hold of it. But one thing I do: Forgetting what is behind and straining toward what is ahead, I <u>press on</u> toward the goal to win the prize for which God has called me heavenward in Christ Jesus. (Philippians 3:13-14, NIV, emphasis added)*

In the face of opposition and persecution, Paul pressed on. As a result, churches began to grow, and the message of the Gospel spread throughout the region. Paul struggled to put his past mistakes behind him, but he strived to look ahead and keep his eyes on the prize. He was steadfast in not letting his past define him, and he was determined to chart a new course for his life.

Paul's perseverance and determination were an inspiration to the early church and new believers. In his visits and letters to them, he regularly had to remind them to press on, hold on, and stand firm in their faith. Because they were all under great opposition and faced stressful and difficult times, Paul became a spiritual cheerleader and champion of their faith.

Surrounded by the culture of the ancient Greek games, Paul used the metaphor of an athlete in training to describe his faith journey and depict the type of discipline needed for the early Christian church to survive and thrive.

Chapter 8

> *Don't you realize that in a race everyone runs, but only one person gets the prize? So run to win! All athletes are disciplined in their training. They do it to win a prize that will fade away, but we do it for an eternal prize. So I run with purpose in every step. I am not just shadowboxing. I discipline my body like an athlete, training it to do what it should. Otherwise, I fear that after preaching to others I myself might be disqualified. (1 Corinthians 9:24-27, NLT)*

Many things in life take perseverance. Following God takes perseverance, and leading well takes perseverance, a lot of perseverance. Over time, our leadership will be tested. At some point, most of our official and unofficial leadership roles take a grit your teeth, buckle down, brace for impact, and hard push forward type of perseverance. That's the nature of the beast. In life, in faith, and in leadership, we must press on with a resilient and forged determination. Otherwise, we may give way to enemies that seek to stop our progress, block our goals, and undermine our purpose. Like Paul, we must hold fast to our faith, train hard, persevere, and run to win.

PASS IT ON

It's hard to win a relay race if you don't pass the baton to the next runner. It sounds silly and basic, but it's true. When I was on the track team, I ran the mile (1600m) relay race. Each team had four runners, and each runner's job was to run one lap as fast as you could; then pass the baton to your teammate. The hand-off was critical. The timing had to be just right, or we would lose time or worse, drop the baton. We practiced it over and over to make sure we made a clean exchange and didn't fumble the hand-off. Many races were won or lost based on a team's ability to execute good hand-offs between runners. Leadership is the same way.

Paul wasn't satisfied with being a good leader himself. He knew the importance of passing on his faith and his leadership to others. To pass on his faith, he contextualized and adapted his methods to meet the needs of the people and the culture around him. He stayed true to his message but tried hard to remove barriers that might keep people from connecting with God. In passing on his leadership, Paul invested in the younger generation of leaders and pastors through his teaching, visiting, and letter writing, especially to the young church leader Timothy.

> *Even though I am a free man with no master, I have become a slave to all people to bring many to Christ. When I was with the Jews, I lived like a Jew to bring the Jews to Christ.... When I am with the Gentiles who do not follow the Jewish law, I too live apart from that law so I can bring them to Christ. But I do not ignore the law of God; I obey the law of Christ.... Yes, I try to find common ground with everyone, doing everything I can to save some. (1 Corinthians 9:19-22, NLT)*

> *This letter is from Paul, chosen by the will of God to be an apostle of Christ Jesus. I have been sent out to tell others about the life he has promised through faith in Christ Jesus. I am writing to Timothy, my dear son.... Hold on to the pattern of wholesome teaching you learned from me—a pattern shaped by the faith and love that you have in Christ Jesus. (2 Timothy 1:1-2a, 13, NLT)*

Leading well means training others to lead well and passing on the torch of leadership to those around us and those under our leadership. In training others to lead well, we multiply our leadership and increase our impact. While training others and passing the torch is a basic aspect of all leadership, it is often not done well. Missed opportunities, lack of effort, inadequate skills, and failed hand-offs litter the leadership landscape and leave teammates to suffer for the poor planning of those in charge. Leading well means taking the time to invest in people properly and making the leadership hand-off at all levels a top priority because it is vital to the longevity of the group, team, squad, or company.

Chapter 8

THE CHANGE: Outcomes + Faith

How does infusing faith into our leadership affect how we view and handle success? Faith redefines success and how we view outcomes in three key ways.

First, faith-based leadership redefines what a successful leader looks like. A faith-based leader pivots his or her leadership toward God and allows Him to shape how we lead others. It can be challenging to realign our leadership styles, strategies, and methods to fit with biblical values, but we must if we are to truly lead well.

Second, faith-based leadership redefines our faithfulness to God as the most important outcome over and above any other leadership metrics. We all have unique leadership goals, important outcomes, and end results that we want to achieve. However, faith-based leadership reframes these measurements of success in light of our individual and collective faithfulness to God first. Leading well means embracing Paul's secret that Christ gives us the strength to do all things.

Third, successful faith-based leaders persevere and pass on their leadership and their faith. In doing so, we ensure the future of our vision and set up our teams for success. Leading well means leaving a legacy of leaders beside and behind us who know how to lead well. Whether it's one or one hundred, find a way to pass on your leadership and your faith. Not every leadership role lends itself to this but try your best to make it happen. The success and future of our leadership depends on it.

LEADERSHIP SPOTLIGHT: THE WRIGHT BROTHERS

My grandfather was an Air Force pilot. He flew C-130 cargo planes and trained other pilots during his time in the military. He had a love for flying gliders and planes, and his name is on display at the National Air & Space Museum for his contributions as an aeronautical engineer. My father, Dan, grew up flying in his dad's glider and shares the following leadership spotlight from the field of aviation.

The Wright brothers grew up in Dayton, Ohio. Wilbur and Orville worked in their father's bicycle shop where they quickly became very good at constructing bicycles with chains and gears. Their interests expanded into designing new inventions like small motors, a printing press, and eventually, they were inspired to build a flying machine.

They researched books, articles, and Smithsonian publications for ideas. Not only did they read about flight, but they also carefully observed birds and noted the change of wing position when they turned or banked. As they studied birds in flight, they got the idea of warping the wings. Will tried to mimic the wing shape by twisting a long bicycle innertube box to get the warping effect. As they experimented with different designs, their mother encouraged them to make the proper calculations and get it right on paper first.[49] So they were taught at an early age to keep a log of their tests, make improvements on paper before building, and use a scientific approach as they experimented with different designs through trial and error.

The brothers designed and tested many wing and airplane designs but were unable to achieve the necessary lift and control to keep the plane in the air. They struggled to get the right amount of lift that the wings needed compared to the opposing forces of drag. At times, they were ridiculed for their ideas and designs, but they pressed on in their work despite the opposition and past failed attempts to fly.

The key to their eventual success was a pivot in their thinking and designs based on two important factors. First, they corrected an error in the lift equation. Second, they developed flight controls for pitch, yaw, and roll. The Wright brothers persevered in testing their new calculations for lift and applied it to wing design. They figured out that the old constant value of (.0054) that had been used for over 100 years was wrong and had been contributing to past failures. Based on their trials with a kite and glider, they lowered the lift calculations and used a new constant of (.0033) for the lift formula.[50]

To aid in their experiments, they built a wind tunnel which was used to test the wing lift before they built it. They tested over 200 wing models which led to longer and narrower wing shapes for the best lift. In about a six-week period, they flew over 1,000 glider flights. For better steering, they developed wing warping to control roll (rotation),

Chapter 8

a forward elevator to control pitch (up/down), and a rear rudder to control yaw (side to side). They even consulted with the U.S. government for the best place to experiment with flights and the best weather conditions. The next step was to build an engine capable of lifting the plane's weight and theirs. After experimentation, they developed an engine that powered two rear propellers and provided the proper thrust.[50]

Finally, on December 17, 1903, at Kill Devil Hills near Kitty Hawk, North Carolina, they made their historic motorized flight. They each flew the prototype airplane: 175 feet by Wilbur and 200 feet by Orville at about 10 feet above ground. The last flight of the day was 852 feet in length and lasted 59 seconds. They tried to publish their flights in the local newspaper and later in scientific magazines but were refused saying the flights were insignificant.[50]

After initial rejections, they continued to persevere in getting their work recognized. They had the foresight as leaders in the field to keep good records, to remain faithful to the scientific process, and to document their work so that it could be duplicated and passed on. Eventually, the Wright brothers were able to secure patents and pursue buyers for their airplane, the "Wright Flyer."

Over time and after a long struggle with competitors and legal red tape, the Wright brothers were able to negotiate with the U.S., France, Britain, and Germany to sell the company and designs. Several years after the initial flights and in large part due to the European interest in the technology, the U.S. Army Signal Corps awarded a contract to the Wrights in 1908. Later, they received another contract from an emerging French company. All in all, they made aviation history. As a result of their success, the Wright brothers are credited with the invention of the powered airplane and the launch of motorized aviation.[50]

The Wright brothers led the way for tremendous breakthroughs in aviation technology. By making motorized flight possible, they changed the world in many ways.

While we don't know the Wright brothers' personal views on faith, their leadership in the field of aviation follows some of Paul's key leadership principles of pivoting, persevering, and passing it on.

The Wright brothers' work redefined successful aviation design and flight mechanics for all those who would follow in their footsteps.

Building a successful airplane is one thing, but being successful as a person and leader is another. It is hard to be a successful leader. The path toward success can be a long and challenging road. It takes a lot of hard work, dedication, and determination. Like building an airplane, leading well takes practice, repetition, experimentation, perseverance, being faithful to the process, passing on our knowledge and skills, and at times a pivot in our thinking.

FROM THE TRENCHES

WHAT DOES IT TAKE TO LEAD WELL IN YOUR LEADERSHIP CONTEXT?

"FLEXIBILITY. IT TAKES BEING VERY FLUID AND FLEXIBLE, BEING ABLE TO CHANGE DIRECTIONS ON A DIME. HOLD TIGHTLY TO THE MISSION, BUT HOLD LOOSELY TO THE MODEL OF MINISTRY BECAUSE CHANGE IS A CONSTANT." [51]

-JACOB NETHERTON: CAMPUS PASTOR
SALTY CHURCH, FLAGLER BEACH, FL

Chapter 8

PUTTING IT INTO PRACTICE:
What does a change in <u>outcomes</u> mean to you?

Before you move on, think about, discuss, and apply the following questions as they relate to your leadership within your company, team, church, school, or family.

Leadership Thoughts

1. What key points stick out to you from this chapter and why?
2. In what ways does your leadership need to pivot toward God and away from other things?
3. How does infusing faith into your leadership affect how you view and handle success?
4. What does it mean to redefine success as faithfulness to God first and to the goals of the company, team, church, family, or school next?
5. How have you had to persevere in your leadership, and how has God provided for you along the way?
6. How can you pass on your leadership to others, and what would it take to do that well?

CHAPTER 9
CHANGE IN CREDIT:
Who Gets the Glory?
Featured Leader: Moses

Leadership can be a tricky thing. If handled poorly, bad decisions and questionable choices can quickly spiral into scandal and corruption. The allure of power, the thirst for fame, and the quest for glory can cause us to compromise our integrity and slip into the dark side of ambition. One of the most infamous leadership and political scandals in the United States was Watergate. Dan shares the following story about Watergate, President Nixon, and John Dean's quest for glory.

The Watergate scandal occurred during Richard Nixon's presidency between 1972-74. The scandal involved three main aspects. First, there was a break-in at the Democratic National Committee headquarters inside the Watergate Office Building located in Washington, D.C. Second, it involved illegal wiretapping or bugging phone lines to spy and gain access to sensitive information. Third, it involved a complex array of cover-ups by many administration officials. The bottom line is that Republican administrators were trying to gain information that would harm the Democratic Party and help the Republican Party get re-elected.[52]

As White House counsel to Richard Nixon, John Dean was one of the primary players in the Watergate scandal. Dean overlooked many things that were illegal because he was focused on the goal of re-election and gaining another four years for the Republicans to be in office. He enjoyed the power and authority he was given and took credit for many of the Watergate events. In his book "Blind Ambition," Dean admitted that he wanted to move up in the leadership hierarchy regardless of the cost. He confessed that he was blinded by his own ambition for power and position.[52]

As more and more incriminating evidence was found about the Watergate break-in, Dean continued to lie and deceive the investigators by hiding the truth. Dean was driven by his desire for power and political significance which culminated in his deep involvement in the crisis around him. From his perspective, Dean asserts that the continuous recognition from the White House made him think he had achieved power and importance only to realize that he was failing. For instance, he states *"I was basking in the glory of being publicly perceived as the man the President had turned to with a nasty problem like Watergate."* [52] Dean enjoyed the attention and went on to say, *"How about that? The President was mentioning my name on national television. That I thought was a real vote of confidence. He was saying I could pull off the cover- up."* [52]

Dean spares no one in his narrative, including himself. He documents his own weaknesses, instances of his opportunism, greed, vanity, and cowardice. He had lost his moral consciousness. Blind to the faults of the President and blind to his own shallow need for advancement, Dean broke the law.

As the incident became more public, there was a shift in Dean's thinking from fame and re-election to the survival of himself and the Nixon administration. Dean only regained his moral vision when it was required to save his own skin. As a result, he ended up being a whistleblower on the entire scandal. Ultimately, John Dean became the government's key witness in the investigations that ended the Nixon presidency. After Nixon's involvement in the cover-up was made public, he resigned from office on August 9, 1974. In the end, Dean suffered the consequences of bad choices and served time in prison.[52]

Years later, after hundreds of hours of White House recordings were made public and many books were written about Watergate, Dean felt the need to set the record straight. In Dean's follow-up book, "Blind Ambition: The End of the Story" he adds a new section

Chapter 9

clarifying how his intent in his original book was to illustrate what he and others did wrong not right. In "The End of the Story" edition, he admits his mistakes and takes responsibility for his misguided ambition.[53]

THE POINT

The quest for personal glory is a dangerous road. Our own ego and desire for fame and fortune can blind us to what's really going on inside our hearts. The desire to be noticed, get credit, and achieve greatness stems from a self-centered perspective and alters our view of reality. We end up thinking too highly of ourselves, and it diminishes our leadership effectiveness. After all, who wants to follow a self-absorbed egotist bent on his or her own advancement? However, pride is not always so obvious. While our own personal battles with ego and pride are usually more subtle than a full-blown scandal, they can still sabotage our leadership. Leading well means keeping our ego in check and not chasing after our own glory.

MOSES' MISTAKE

There are important leadership lessons that we can learn from Moses including a big mistake he made along the way. We can see these lessons in five key ways through his role as a <u>servant</u> of the Lord, his <u>status</u> as God's chosen mediator, his <u>shift</u> in thinking, as <u>sin</u> creeps into his heart, and how he must <u>suffer</u> the consequences.

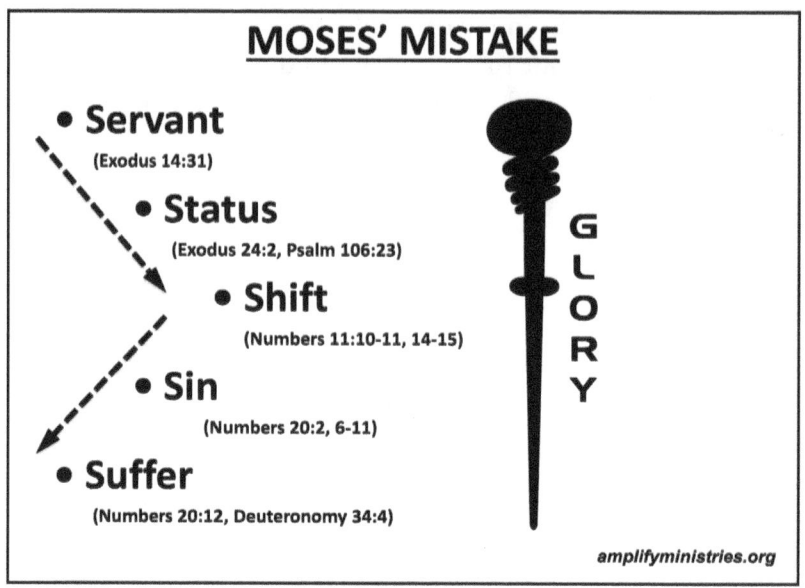

SERVANT OF THE LORD

The story of Moses' life has an interesting path. He was a Hebrew born in captivity and raised in Egypt. As an adult, he fled from the Egyptians to Midian and started a family. Later in life, Moses was called by God to go back to Egypt and free his people, the Israelites, from slavery. Moses was a reluctant leader, but he eventually agreed to serve the Lord and lead the people out of Egypt.

> *When the people of Israel saw the mighty power that the LORD had unleashed against the Egyptians, they were filled with awe before him. They put their faith in the LORD and in his servant Moses. (Exodus 14:31, NLT)*

In helping free the people of Israel from slavery in Egypt, Moses had earned the people's respect. After they witnessed God using Moses to part the Red Sea and escape from Pharaoh's armies, the people of Israel could tell that Moses had God's favor. They trusted Moses to lead them as God's servant.

Chapter 9

Sometimes leadership must be earned. It takes time to build trust with the people we are leading, especially in a new role. Even though God had called him to lead, Moses still needed the people's trust and respect, because without it they would not follow him for very long. To lead well, the people who follow us need to see our commitment to helping them, see that we really care, and see our faith in action.

STATUS AS GOD'S CHOSEN MEDIATOR

Moses was God's chosen representative to act as a mediator between God and the people of Israel. Moses had a special role and connection with God that at times gained him status with the people and at other times made the people afraid of him. As the chosen mediator, Moses bore the responsibility of communicating God's instructions to the people, intervening on the people's behalf, and helping them follow God. Moses' role was similar to acting as the moderator or negotiator between two legal parties.

> *"Only Moses is allowed to come near to the LORD. The others must not come near, and none of the other people are allowed to climb up the mountain with him." (Exodus 24:2, NLT)*

> *When Moses came down Mount Sinai carrying the two stone tablets inscribed with the terms of the covenant, he wasn't aware that his face had become radiant because he had spoken to the LORD. So when Aaron and the people of Israel saw the radiance of Moses' face, they were afraid to come near him. (Exodus 34:29-30, NLT)*

Being God's chosen mediator was a heavy responsibility and a dangerous one. At times, Moses had to step in when the people messed up and begged God for their very lives. It was not easy having to navigate what God was asking and commanding the people to do and dealing with the divided loyalties, sins, and whims of the people of

Israel. In many ways, Moses was an ambassador for God and a diplomatic advocate for the people.

> ... But Moses, his chosen one, stepped between the LORD and the people. He begged him to turn from his anger and not destroy them. (Psalm 106:23b, NLT)

Without Moses' leadership and faith, the people of Israel probably would have died many times over, either from Pharaoh's army, God's punishment, or their own stupidity. The people's need for an advocate was clear. In this way, Moses' role as mediator foreshadowed Jesus' future role as our ultimate mediator before God (1 Timothy 2:5). As the people of Israel entered a special covenant relationship with God as his chosen people, they needed to keep the ten commandments and follow God's instructions or risk breaking their part of the covenant. However, they lacked the wisdom to govern themselves well and were often incapable, forgetful, or unwilling to keep God's commands. That's why they needed a leader.

SHIFT IN THINKING

As a leader, do you ever get tired of the people you are leading? Do the people you lead, supervise, train, and develop ever get on your nerves? Do you ever feel like the people under your leadership don't appreciate who you are and what you do for them? Do you ever get tired of their complaining, their repeated mistakes, and their short-sightedness? I do.

It is not easy leading people. Parents get frustrated with their kids for not listening. Coaches get annoyed by the repeated mistakes of their team. Managers get irritated with their employees' incompetence. Executives get ticked at their companies' unwillingness to change. Students get bothered by their peers' immaturity. The list could go on and on, but one thing is clear. Leading others can be frustrating at times.

Well, Moses was feeling many of those frustrations in a big way. The seeds of his frustration began when he came down the mountain with the Ten Commandments only to find the people of

Chapter 9

Israel worshiping a golden calf they had just made instead of worshiping God.

> *When they came near the camp, Moses saw the calf and the dancing, and he burned with anger. He threw the stone tablets to the ground, smashing them at the foot of the mountain. He took the calf they had made and burned it. Then he ground it into powder, threw it into the water, and forced the people to drink it. (Exodus 32:19-20, NLT)*

Moses' frustration with the people of Israel grew as they wandered in the desert. After God used him to free them from slavery in Egypt, they complained about the food, the wandering, and Moses' leadership. Their complaining was so aggravating and ridiculous that God got angry, Moses wanted to die, and the people wished they were back in Egypt.

> *Moses heard all the families standing in the doorways of their tents whining, and the LORD became extremely angry. Moses was also very aggravated. And Moses said to the LORD, "Why are you treating me, your servant, so harshly? Have mercy on me! What did I do to deserve the burden of all these people? …. I can't carry all these people by myself! The load is far too heavy! If this is how you intend to treat me, just go ahead and kill me. Do me a favor and spare me this misery!" (Numbers 11:10-11, 14-15, NLT)*

> *Then the whole community began weeping aloud, and they cried all night. Their voices rose in a great chorus of protest against Moses and Aaron. "If only we had died in Egypt, or even here in the wilderness!" they complained. (Numbers 14:1-2, NLT)*

What happens when the shepherd gets sick and tired of leading the stubborn and stinky sheep? His thinking begins to shift.

He starts focusing on himself and his own frustrations. He questions his leadership role and the worthiness of those he leads. For Moses, his heart and mind began to drift. He had reached his limit with the people of Israel, and he was sick and tired of their complaining and accusations. Moses' thinking shifted inward, and it opened the door for sin.

SIN CREEPS IN

The people of Israel rebelled against Moses because there was no water to drink. They had forgotten how God provided water for them before and were complaining once more (Exodus 17:5-6). Again, Moses took the blame, and his frustration continued to mount. He turned to the Lord, and God gave him a solution. God gave Moses very specific instructions to follow and planned to miraculously provide the people with water from a rock.

> *There was no water for the people to drink at that place, so they rebelled against Moses and Aaron.... Moses and Aaron turned away from the people and went to the entrance of the Tabernacle, where they fell face down on the ground. Then the glorious presence of the LORD appeared to them, and the LORD said to Moses, "You and Aaron must take the staff and assemble the entire community. As the people watch, <u>speak to the rock</u> over there, and it will pour out its water. You will provide enough water from the rock to satisfy the whole community and their livestock."*
>
> *So Moses did as he was told. He took the staff from the place where it was kept before the LORD. Then he and Aaron summoned the people to come and gather at the rock. "Listen, you rebels!" he shouted. "Must we bring you water from this rock?" Then Moses raised his hand and <u>struck the rock twice</u> with the staff, and water gushed out. So the entire community and their*

Chapter 9

> *livestock drank their fill. (Numbers 20:2, 6-11, NLT, emphasis added)*

Did Moses obey God's instructions completely? No. Instead of speaking to the rock, Moses struck the rock with his staff. It may seem small or incidental, but it is not. So, what's the big deal? In striking the rock, Moses took credit for the miracle that God did. In that moment, Moses decided to flex his power in front of the people; the power that God had given him. He took the honor intended for God, and he took it for himself. In doing so, he sinned and committed a huge leadership mistake; a mistake for which he was later punished. Out of frustration with the people, he elevated himself and took the glory.

Leading well requires that we do battle with our pride and selfishness and give the glory to God. In our work as leaders, we must give God the glory for the leadership ability He has given us and point to Him in our success. If we don't handle the frustrations of leadership wisely, they will grow within us, leaving us open to critical mistakes and sinful actions.

On a practical level, I believe it is important to give credit where credit is due. Nobody likes glory hogs. If your team or teammates do well, share the credit with them. If your company is successful, share the credit with your employees. If your ministry succeeds, share the credit with your members and volunteers. People need to feel appreciated, but ultimate credit must be reserved for the God who made us and gave us the abilities we have in the first place.

SUFFER THE CONSEQUENCES

Sin has consequences. Moses had to pay the price for disobeying God, and the price was heavy. Because he took credit for God's miracle, Moses was not allowed to enter the Promised Land. It was a hard consequence for Moses because they had been wandering in the desert and waiting for the Promised Land for many years. Not being allowed to enter the land was tough. It's sort of like he didn't get to cross the finish line, and that's a hard thing to swallow as a leader. In some ways, it may even seem unfair.

> *But the LORD said to Moses and Aaron, "Because you did not trust in me enough to honor me as holy in the sight of the Israelites, you will not bring this community into the land I give them." (Numbers 20:12, NIV)*

> *Then Moses climbed Mount Nebo from the plains of Moab to the top of Pisgah, across from Jericho. There the LORD showed him the whole land... Then the LORD said to him, "This is the land I promised on oath to Abraham, Isaac and Jacob when I said, 'I will give it to your descendants.' I have let you see it with your eyes, but you will not cross over into it." (Deuteronomy 34:1a, 4, NIV)*

To soften the blow, God showed Moses an act of kindness and allowed him to see the land from a mountain top. However, the honor of taking the people into the Promised Land was given to Joshua instead. I am sure that Moses felt blessed to see the land of promise from afar, but not as good as taking the people there himself.

It is hard to face the consequences of our leadership mistakes. Sometimes those consequences just affect the person in charge. More often they affect everyone in, around, and under that person's leadership. Leaders aren't perfect; they make mistakes from time to time. However, leading well requires us to own our mistakes, and work hard to avoid them in the first place by taking steps to address our weaknesses.

THE CHANGE: Credit + Faith

How does infusing faith into our leadership affect how credit is given? Faith redistributes the credit and who gets the glory in three key ways.

First, faith-based leadership gives God the glory in all things. Leading well is not about personal glory, individual advancement, or achievement. The wise leader takes the compliments, praise, success, approval, and fame and publicly points to God and privately lifts them up to the Lord at the end of the day with gratitude.

Second, infusing faith into our leadership requires a humble heart. Leaders who embrace their own humility, swallow their pride, and lift others up are easy to appreciate and follow. Letting go of our ego is not easy, but it helps build unity and trust.

Third, faith-based leadership shares the credit with others. Leading well is about helping others succeed, elevating those around you, putting them in the spotlight, and winning as a team. The buffet of shared success is far sweeter and more satisfying than a single dish of pride eaten alone.

LEADERSHIP SPOTLIGHT: THE RISE AND FALL OF VEGGIETALES

VeggieTales and Big Idea Productions started as a company that made animated kids' videos about Bible stories using talking vegetables. For a time, they became wildly popular as the iconic Bob the Tomato and Larry the Cucumber hosted each episode. Using creative cartoons to share biblical truths with kids was a great idea. In fact, my kids and my family owned and enjoyed many of the VeggieTales stories. A while back, I heard the founder of VeggieTales, Phil Vischer, speak at a conference about the rise and fall of his company.

> *"VeggieTales was an enormous success. It was a dream come true.... God was using our efforts. Lives were being touched. So, I decided I should get busier. We could do even more good. We started producing books, records, computer games, toys, a live touring show, shows at theme parks, and even our own feature film. I figured if I could have this much impact just making videos, think of the impact I could have if I built the next Disney. Of course, I realized that would make me the next Walt; I kind of liked the sound of that....*

LEADERSHIP REBORN

Turns out, so did a lot of other people. I met with the artists from Disney and DreamWorks and Warner Brothers and some of them thought 'Hey, he could be the next Walt' and they wanted to sign up for the ride. So, I hired all of them and put them to work on all the projects I set into motion. By the year 2000, we had gone from three people to more than 200; the biggest animation studio between the coasts....

Right about then, everything started to go wrong. The management team I'd put together to grow the company did a wonderful job hiring a whole mess of people, but they couldn't get along with each other and they couldn't get along with me.... And then without warning our sales stopped growing....

In April of 2000, I realized that everything I'd built was in very real danger of falling apart, and I realized I had to do something that I'd promised myself and others I would never do. I had to let people go. So, from 210 to 180 to 140 to 100, every layoff broke my heart....

And while all that was happening, we were taken to court by a former distributor.... Walking out of court that day I knew it was over... I knew Big Idea would have no choice but to go into bankruptcy and that everything that I had built in the prior fourteen years- every character I had created, every story I had written, every song I had written would be sold at auction to the highest bidder to pay as much of our debt as possible....

I had no idea how God could just stand back from something that was doing so much good and watch it fall apart.... And then I started hearing His whispers... I got an email from a woman I had never met, who I

Chapter 9

> *don't believe had ever met me. She started by thanking me for my amazing work and praising the impact we were having, but then she closed her email by saying 'but keep an eye on your pride'.... I realized that my good work had become an idol that defined me. Rather than finding my identity in God, I was finding it in my immense drive to do good work....*
>
> *After Big Idea fell apart and all the leftover pieces including many of my friends were swept up and moved to Nashville by the new owners, I spent some time hurting; just hurting.... (I realized) the most important thing is not the work I can do for God. The most important thing is to make God the most important thing."* [54]

Unfortunately, VeggieTales was never the same after that. As Phil Vischer shared how his dream fell apart and how his pride got the best of him, the audience he was speaking to was moved and honored by his openness. Losing his company was certainly a painful lesson in humility as pride is a slippery slope. Even so, he is not the first leader to fall into that trap. Many political leaders, athletes, actors, music artists, and church leaders have fallen due to their pride. Cultivating a humble heart is not easy, but it is a much-needed leadership quality as fame and success beckons us to believe too highly in ourselves.

It can be incredibly rewarding and fulfilling to do things for God, to be used by God, and to make a difference for God's kingdom. However, our success can cause us to lose focus like Moses and make the critical leadership mistake of taking the credit for ourselves or taking our focus off God. There is a danger in our leadership journey of crossing the line and shifting our focus from building God's kingdom to building our own. To lead well, we need to continually give God the glory and keep our eyes fixed on Him.

FROM THE TRENCHES
What does it take to lead well in your leadership context?

"Leading students well takes transparency, love, urgency, and vision. In order to build effective relationships with students, you have to be open and honest with them and show genuine love. Next, urgency is critical in leading and investing in teenagers. Giving teenagers a vision to grab onto and then build on it with intentionality is crucial to engaging students on their level and building them up for the future." [55]

-Matthew Ranck
Student Pastor at Crescent Beach Baptist

Chapter 9

SECTION SUMMARY

Great job finishing up the eight fundamentals that change when we infuse our leadership with faith. Here's what's coming up next in part three: Enemies to Faith-Based Leadership and how we can overcome them.

- The Enemy of Our Faith: Satan
- The Enemy's Domain: The World
- The Enemy Within: Adam
- Victory Over the Enemy: You

We also have some great illustrations coming up, including: movie plot twists, Italian architecture, NASCAR racing, boxing, temptations, coloring page conundrum, rust, would you rather quiz, and stress tips.

PUTTING IT INTO PRACTICE:
What does a change in <u>credit</u> mean to you?

Before you move on, think about, discuss, and apply the following questions as they relate to your leadership within your company, team, church, school, or family.

Leadership Thoughts

1. What key points stick out to you from this chapter and why?
2. Have you ever had success and been tempted to take the credit and the glory for yourself, to brag, to boast, to show off, or to think too highly of yourself? Explain.
3. How often do you give God the glory and share the credit with the people you lead?
4. How do you handle things when the people you lead frustrate you and don't want to follow you?
5. What would being a servant leader who gives God the glory look like in your leadership context?
6. Describe a time when your pride got in the way of leading well. How could a humbler approach have been helpful?

PART 3
ENEMIES TO FAITH-BASED LEADERSHIP

A BRIEF EXPLANATION

There are many enemies and obstacles to our leadership, but faith-based leadership identifies our most formidable foe. In the cosmic battle of good versus evil, God is on one side and Satan is on the other. Jesus is the heroic protagonist, and Satan is the villainous antagonist. The powers of light versus the forces of darkness. In this epic saga, these two rivals are fighting for the hearts, lives, and devotion of the people of earth. However, the playing field is not even. Everyone is born into darkness and sin and therefore must choose the light. It sounds like an intriguing fantasy novel, but it's not. It's an insidious conflict that we have all been thrust into, and it paints a challenging backdrop for us to pursue any kind of good leadership. But that's even more reason why we need faith-based leaders to rise up and lead the way.

I realize that a chapter on Satan and the spiritual opposition to our leadership can be disturbing, a bit scary, and depressing. However, that's not the intent. The goal is to help prepare you as a leader for the battles you may face and to identify our seldom talked about and rarely understood enemy. Be encouraged that we have a mighty God who is more powerful than our enemy, and that the Lord fights on our behalf.

CHAPTER 10
THE ENEMY OF OUR FAITH
Featured Leader: Satan

In any battle, game, match-up, or challenge, it is helpful for us to know our opponent and evaluate our enemy. Gathering intelligence, counter-surveillance, and strategic information about our opponent can help us come up with an effective battle plan and protect us from making critical mistakes. To that end, this chapter is designed to help you understand the enemy of our faith, identify key areas of the battlefield, and recognize some of his battle tactics and strategies.

Not everyone believes that we have a spiritual enemy trying to undermine our lives and our leadership. However, it's true. The Bible makes it clear that Satan is a predator and wants to keep people from following God. Therefore, if you desire to follow God, lead well, and infuse your faith into your leadership, then be aware and on guard that Satan is your enemy because he is God's enemy.

Make no mistake, Satan is a leader. Not a good one, mind you, but an incredibly effective one; villains often are. He is intelligent, organized, strategic, crafty, deceptive, ruthless, powerful, and dangerous. While Satan is a fallen angel, he has become a fierce and menacing adversary. Even so, his power and reach are limited, and his fate has already been decided. In the end, God wins, and Satan and his forces are defeated and punished for all eternity. Until that happens, we live in the in-between time and must do battle against the forces of darkness in our world and in our hearts.

For our struggle is not against flesh and blood, but against the rulers, against the authorities, against the powers of this dark world and against the spiritual forces of evil in the heavenly realms. (Ephesians 6:12, NIV)

SATAN'S DECEPTION

There are very revealing leadership principles that we can learn from the tactics and strategies of Satan and his command of the forces of darkness. We can see these principles in key ways in his <u>deceiving</u> the world, <u>distorting</u> the truth, <u>delivering</u> temptation, <u>developing</u> darkness, and his goal of <u>destroying</u> humanity.

SATAN'S DECEPTION

- **Deceiving the World**
  - (Revelation 12:7-9)
- **Distorting the Truth**
  - (John 8:44)
- **Delivering Temptation**
  - (Matthew 4:1, 1 Thessalonians 3:5)
- **Developing Darkness**
  - (Ephesians 2:2, 2 Corinthians 4:4)
- **Destroying Humanity**
  - (Revelation 9:11, 12:17, 1 Peter 5:8)

amplifyministries.org

DECEIVING THE WORLD

Have you ever watched a movie with a plot twist? At a critical point in the story, it is revealed that one of the main characters has been deceiving people. Perhaps the audience gasps aloud as the plot thickens, the reality of their duplicity sinks in, and the emotion of anger rises toward this unexpected villain.

Chapter 10

In case you need me to jog your memory, here are some classic movie deceptions and betrayals:

- **Lord of the Rings: Fellowship of the Ring**
  Boromir betrays Frodo and tries to take the ring
- **Murder on the Orient Express**
  Agatha Christie's detective Poirot reveals the killer
- **Avatar**
  Jake deceives Neytiri and the Na'vi by pretending to be a native
- **Pirates of the Caribbean: Dead Man's Chest**
  Elizabeth locks Jack to the mast to escape the Kraken
- **Fast and Furious 8: The Fate of the Furious**
  Dom Toretto goes rogue and betrays his crew
- **Mission Impossible**
  Ethan Hunt is set up and betrayed by his boss, the use of masks
- **Star Wars V: The Empire Strikes Back**
  Lando Calrissian betrays Han Solo to Darth Vader and Boba Fett
- **The Matrix**
  Reality is a deception, Cypher sabotages the team
- **Iron Man**
  Family friend, Obadiah Stane betrays Stark and tries to kill him
- **Indiana Jones and The Last Crusade**
  The spy, Elsa Schneider, betrays Jones with a kiss
- **The Passion**
  Judas' betrayal of Jesus

Many movies use deception to infiltrate the opposing forces. Here's an example:

> "It's a regular occurrence in undercover-agent pictures. In order to infiltrate a criminal organization, our hero must befriend an underling, gain their trust... and ultimately stab them in the back in order to complete the elaborate bust." [56]

However, what if we invert this scenario to fit our context?

> *"To infiltrate God's creation, the anti-hero (Satan) must befriend the people of earth, gain their trust...and ultimately stab them in the back in order to complete the deception of the entire world and drag them all down with him."*

The reality is that there is a deception currently going on in the world and Satan is the one trying to deceive all of us. Satan is perhaps running the biggest scam and deception of all time. He started by deceiving Adam and Eve into disobeying God. He continues to deceive the rest of us into believing God doesn't exist, doesn't care, or isn't worth following. Satan wants us to doubt, question, and abandon our faith.

Furthermore, he has deceived people into believing he doesn't exist. What better tactic is there than to get the opposing forces to think their enemy isn't real or isn't a threat. Be careful in your thinking, so that you are not deceived by the enemy.

> *Then there was war in heaven. Michael and his angels fought against the dragon and his angels. And the dragon lost the battle, and he and his angels were forced out of heaven. This great dragon—the ancient serpent called the devil, or Satan, the one deceiving the whole world—was thrown down to the earth with all his angels. (Revelation 12:7-9, NLT)*

> *...But woe to the earth and the sea, because the devil has gone down to you! He is filled with fury, because he knows that his time is short. (Revelation 12:12b, NIV)*

Deception and betrayal make interesting plot twists, but people don't like to be deceived in real life. Be aware that Satan pretends to be an angel of light, but he is an evil deceiver. Faith-based leadership acknowledges that we have a real spiritual enemy, learns to recognize the enemy's deception, and exposes his lies. Faith-based leaders hold fast to their faith in God, seek the wisdom of trusted

Chapter 10

leaders, identify deceptions when they arise, and help others see the enemy's deceptions in their own lives.

DISTORTING THE TRUTH

As we consider some of the tactics of our enemy, deception and distorting the truth go hand in hand. While Satan is a deceiver, he is also called the father of lies for good reason. From lying and deceiving Adam and Eve in the Garden of Eden to distorting the truth while tempting Jesus in the wilderness, Satan has been a liar from the beginning. His main tactics include whispering lies into our ears, tempting us to believe wrong things about ourselves, tempting us to question God and doubt the Bible, convincing us to abandon our faith, twisting the truth, and distorting our perception. The scary thing is, he is really good at it.

In speaking to the religious leaders and unbelieving people who are trying to kill Him, Jesus says the following revealing words about them and the nature of Satan.

> *You belong to your father, the devil, and you want to carry out your father's desires. He was a murderer from the beginning, not holding to the truth, for there is no truth in him. When he lies, he speaks his native language, for he is a liar and the father of lies. (John 8:44, NIV)*

Satan is a master at deception and an expert at lying. That's part of what makes him a formidable villain. These aren't good qualities of a leader, but they are powerful weapons in his arsenal. He has a sneaky way of making wrong things seem right and right things seem wrong. He is also really good at underselling the consequences and getting us to believe that our sinful actions, thoughts, and choices aren't that big of a deal. That's a lie; the truth is that sin is a big deal. Don't fall for his tricks, expose the lies for what they are, and hold on to the truth of God's Word. Keep living and leading with integrity and honor.

DELIVERING TEMPTATION

Temptations come in many forms. Satan and his forces are great at dressing up sin in all kinds of appealing ways. Chocolate-covered lies and dazzling deceptions taste sweet at first; then they burn. The enemy plays on our appetites, knows our weaknesses, and offers up a poison apple at just the right time. In the blink of an eye, we exchange a moment of pleasure for a slow death. Before we know it, we are in a world of hurt and stuck in a life of slavery to sinful addictions.

> *Then Jesus was led by the Spirit into the wilderness to be tempted there by the devil. (Matthew 4:1, NLT)*

> *... I sent Timothy to find out whether your faith was still strong. I was afraid that the tempter had gotten the best of you and that our work had been useless. (1 Thessalonians 3:5b, NLT)*

The temptation to lie about what happened, cheat on the test, bend the rules, steal money, look at inappropriate images online, sleep around, sneak a drink, or get a quick drug fix can be addictive and hard to stop. The temptation to explode in anger, lash out in violence, curse and swear, falsely accuse others, take advantage of others, place a bet, overindulge in shopping, eat too much, starve ourselves, or find cheap escapes from our problems can be difficult to resist. Even the best leaders can struggle with these types of temptations.

Often, faith-based leaders are prone to the enemy's attacks. All of the biblical leaders we have discussed faced temptations. Some gave in to the temptations and some stood firm in their faith.

Chapter 10

GAVE IN

- **David**: tempted and committed adultery
  - *2 Samuel 11:1-5*
- **Abraham**: tempted to doubt and made his own plan
  - *Genesis 16:1-4*
- **Moses**: tempted and took credit for God's miracle
  - *Numbers 20:6-12*

STOOD FIRM

- **Jesus**: tempted by Satan in the desert
  - *Matthew 4:1-11*
- **Nehemiah**: tempted to stop building
  - *Nehemiah 6:1-4*
- **Joseph**: tempted to be with his boss's wife
  - *Genesis 39:8-12*
- **Joshua**: tempted to be afraid and not lead
  - *Joshua 1:6-9*
- **Paul**: tempted to give up
  - *2 Corinthians 11:24-28*

The temptations we face are powerful, but they can be overcome. God promises to provide a way out or a way to resist them if we seek Him through prayer, through Scripture, and by paying attention to His guidance.

> *If you think you are standing strong, be careful not to fall. The temptations in your life are no different from what others experience. And God is faithful. He will not allow the temptation to be more than you can stand. When you are tempted, he will show you a way out so that you can endure. (1 Corinthians 10:12-13, NLT)*

> *And don't let us yield to temptation, but rescue us from the evil one. (Matthew 6:13, NLT)*

However, knowing how to resist isn't enough, we still must choose the way out and flee from the situation. Faith-based leadership learns to recognize the enemy's tactics and takes steps to protect ourselves and our leadership from temptations. Leading well means choosing to resist the temptations we face, asking trusted friends to hold us accountable, and seeking forgiveness when we make mistakes.

DEVELOPING DARKNESS

When you were young, were you afraid of the dark? I was. I liked to keep the nightlight on or a flashlight on hand. I was especially afraid of going down into the dark basement alone. Darkness has a way of giving people the creeps, and for good reason. A lot of shady stuff happens at night and in the dark. In fact, an article from U.S. News and World Report states: *"While most crime takes place during daylight hours, serious crimes are more commonplace at night, a study finds…. The exception is the weekend, when the majority of all kinds of crime take place at night."* [57] Whether it's physical darkness or spiritual darkness, the bottom line is this: darkness breeds dark behavior.

Our enemy and his tactics thrive in darkness. The forces of darkness are called that for a reason. Satan's forces are really good at covert operations and developing darkness within us. They oppose the light and actively try to avoid being exposed. Sin grows in the dark and thrives in secret. Most people try to hide their most sinful behaviors and addictions and pursue them in private. One of the enemy's tactics is to keep us isolated and in the dark, struggling in secret and all alone. The more we give in to sin, the more the darkness and shame grow within us, and the more disconnected from God we become.

> *You used to live in sin, just like the rest of the world, obeying the devil—the commander of the powers in the unseen world. He is the spirit at work in the hearts of those who refuse to obey God. (Ephesians 2:2, NLT)*
>
> *Satan, who is the god of this world, has blinded the minds of those who don't believe. They are unable to*

Chapter 10

see the glorious light of the Good News. They don't understand this message about the glory of Christ, who is the exact likeness of God. (2 Corinthians 4:4, NLT)

Satan develops darkness in and around us to the point it blinds us from the truth, distorts our thinking, derails our perspective, disrupts our progress, and blocks our vision. The darkness becomes so heavy that we can't find our way or see the light. If we are not careful, the darkness can consume us. We can get stuck in sin, drift away from God, and allow our faith to fade.

To illustrate the point even further, there is a great conversation about the power of darkness in Marvel's sci-fi series "Agents of S.H.I.E.L.D." When the enhanced female agent, Daisy, is isolated and full of pain and rage her friend and fellow agent, Mack, says to her: *"You know what? Another thing the devil's capable of... filling a person with so much anger and so many dark thoughts that is consumes them. But it's up to that individual to make a choice. Either let the darkness fester and grow or let the light inside shine through and vanquish the darkness."* [58]

Faith-based leadership fights the darkness and resists the drift to the dark side. Leading well means living in the light and shining the light of God's Word on the dark areas of our lives. Faith-based leaders push back the darkness with the light of Christ and seek to help others out of the darkness.

DESTROYING HUMANITY

War often causes destruction. Destroyed cities, destroyed armies, and devastated countries are the result of many hard-fought battles across time and around the world. We live in a dangerous world with real physical enemies, but we also live in a world with unseen spiritual enemies. Most people don't realize that our world is at war. The battlefield isn't necessarily a strategic piece of land, and the battle plan isn't the traditional siege of a capital city. Much of the battlefield takes place in the spiritual realm and in the hearts and minds of each person. Satan the Destroyer is actively opposing the people of God, the plans of God, and the purposes of God. He wants to destroy our lives, our leadership, and our loyalty to God.

> *Their king is the angel from the bottomless pit; his name in Hebrew is Abaddon, and in Greek, Apollyon—the Destroyer. (Revelation 9:11, NLT)*

> *And the dragon was angry at the woman and declared war against the rest of her children—all who keep God's commandments and maintain their testimony for Jesus. (Revelation 12:17, NLT)*

Keep in mind, the devil is a fallen angel who was kicked out of heaven along with those loyal to him. He leads the demonic forces of darkness in rebellion against God. Ultimately, he wants to overthrow God's kingdom and be worshiped as a god. He wants to destroy the followers of God and the work of God. He uses devious tactics to corrupt the hearts of men and women and push them, pull them, trap them, trick them, or sway them to the dark side. He takes many forms and is described as an angry dragon, crafty serpent, attacking lion, accusing lawyer, commanding ruler, and a pretender who masquerades as an angel of light.

> *Be alert and of sober mind. Your enemy the devil prowls around like a roaring lion looking for someone to devour. (1 Peter 5:8, NIV)*

> *Put on all of God's armor so that you will be able to stand firm against all strategies of the devil. (Ephesians 6:11, NLT)*

So how do we combat such an enemy bent on our destruction? Thankfully, Jesus Christ is our champion, the Holy Spirit gives us power, the Father has a plan, the Bible is our weapon, faith is our shield, prayer is our provision, and the forces of light are fighting on our behalf. Even so, we each still need to do our part to be on guard, alert, self-controlled, clothed in God's armor, courageous, righteous, full of love, wise, and steadfast in our faith.

THE RUB:
Spiritual Opposition

How does infusing faith into our leadership affect how we view and handle opposition? Faith redefines the battlefield and helps us identify the real enemy in three key ways.

First, we look inward. With a little self-evaluation, we can ask ourselves some enlightening questions: Are there any areas of our life and leadership where the enemy of our faith might be lurking? Are there any ways that we are being deceived? Is the truth hidden or covered up? In what ways are we being tempted? Is darkness getting a foothold anywhere? In what ways is the enemy trying to destroy your leadership, your character, and your effectiveness?

Second, we look outward. Are there external factors opposing your leadership? If so, what are they? With a little team evaluation, we can ask some enlightening questions: Are there any areas of your company, team, church, school, or family where the enemy might be lurking? Are there deceptions, lies, temptations, darkness, or destructive forces within your organization, team, or family? In what ways is the enemy trying to destroy the people you lead, disrupt your team, and halt their effectiveness?

Third, we become discerning. Not all opposition to our leadership is spiritual, but some of it is. Sometimes we face traditional obstacles to leading like: poor communication, lack of planning, unclear expectations, personality conflicts, lack of vision, unqualified people, bad training, and shifting economics. At other times, our leadership and the people we lead can be under fire from the enemy. This is especially true regarding personal issues and sinful behavior like: greed, pride, selfishness, power, control, ambition, jealousy, envy, anger, unresolved conflicts, unforgiveness, lying, and stealing. Faith-based leadership learns to see the difference between traditional obstacles and spiritual opposition and takes steps to address these enemies appropriately.

LEADERSHIP SPOTLIGHT
AN INSIDE LOOK

Most followers of God, especially those in any kind of ministry, can share stories about the spiritual opposition they have experienced in their faith journey and in their leadership roles. When we try to lead well, live right, and serve the Lord, there is opposition. I have experienced strong spiritual opposition in many ways over the years ranging from:

- Personal struggles
- Health issues
- Parenting issues
- Kids acting out
- Troubled students
- Marriage conflicts
- Job difficulties
- Family drama
- Work conflicts
- Financial problems
- Technology disruptions
- Communication breakdowns
- House and cars breaking down
- Blocked pathways and closed doors
- People actively plotting against us
- City opposes church construction
- Difficult board members
- Frustrations and misunderstandings
- Trouble sleeping and bad dreams
- Unanswered prayers... and more

While many of these things are commonplace, I would argue that the timing, frequency, intensity, cause, and destructive effects were the result of significant spiritual attacks surrounding something my family or I was trying to do for God. While that's not always the case; sometimes life just stinks. However, the opposition is real and there are unseen forces trying to undermine us and sabotage our lives and leadership.

Again, I realize that chapters on Satan and the spiritual opposition to our leadership can be disturbing, a bit scary, and depressing. However, that's not the intent. The goal is to help prepare you as a leader for the battles you may face and to identify our seldom talked about and rarely understood enemy. Be encouraged that we have a mighty God who is more powerful than our enemy, and that the Lord fights on our behalf.

Chapter 10

> **FROM THE TRENCHES**
> WHAT DOES IT TAKE TO LEAD WELL IN YOUR LEADERSHIP CONTEXT?
>
> "To overcome spiritual opposition in any context, it only makes sense to draw on spiritual resources. The Bible makes it clear in Ephesians 6 that our spiritual weapons are the Word of God and prayer. I use the illumination of Scripture and the power of prayer to overcome and have victory through the Holy Spirit."
>
> -Tim Ehrhart
> International Missions Strategist:
> HS Ministry at CRU [59]

PUTTING IT INTO PRACTICE

Before you move on, think about, discuss, and apply the following questions as they relate to your leadership within your company, team, church, school, or family.

Leadership Thoughts

1. What key points stick out to you from this chapter and why?
2. In what ways have you faced spiritual opposition in your faith journey and in your leadership roles?
3. How does the harsh reality of a spiritual enemy affect how you lead?
4. Look inward: What areas of your life might the enemy be hiding, deceiving, tempting, or disrupting your leadership effectiveness?
5. Look outward: What external factors, deceptions, behaviors, temptations, darkness, or destructive forces might be disrupting your organization, team, or family?
6. Be discerning: What steps do you need to take to evaluate and address the traditional obstacles and spiritual opposition to your leadership?

CHAPTER 11

THE ENEMY'S DOMAIN:
The World

Featured Leader: Satan

There are very insightful leadership principles that we can learn from how Satan has shaped the worldly environment we live in and in which his forces operate. We can see how he has distorted our perspective through our worldly culture, society's worldly values, people's worldly focus, individual's worldly motives, and our collective worldly pace. Over time, we can be fooled into building our lives on the wrong foundation. As a result, we end up thinking the wrong things; we focus on the wrong things; we want the wrong things; and we chase the wrong things.

SATAN'S DOMAIN
- **Worldly Culture**
  - Wrong Foundation (Matthew 7:24-27)
- **Worldly Values**
  - Wrong Thinking (Romans 1:28-32, 12:2)
- **Worldly Focus**
  - Wrong Priorities (Matthew 16:26, 6:33)
- **Worldly Motives**
  - Wrong Intentions (James 4:2-4)
- **Worldly Pace**
  - Wrong Speed (Exodus 20:8-10a, Psalm 46:10)

amplifyministries.org

WORLDLY CULTURE:
Wrong Foundation

In construction, building a strong and level foundation is critical. The whole project depends on it; just ask the builders of the Leaning Tower of Pisa. This crooked tower in Italy serves as an embarrassing reminder of how important it is to have a good foundation. *"Despite various attempts to reinforce it, Pisa's tower continued to subside at a rate of some 0.05 inches per year, placing it in increasing danger of collapse. By 1990, it was leaning 5.5 degrees (or some 15 feet) from the perpendicular—the most extreme angle yet."* [60] While the ancient marble tower continues to be a site for tourism, its unstable foundation has made it infamous and unsafe.

In a similar way, Satan has helped shape our worldly culture in such a way that many people's lives are crooked and falling apart because they have been fooled into building their lives on the wrong foundation. If I asked you, "Does the current culture of the world promote the things of God?" How would you respond? What kinds of things does the current culture promote? Typically, popular culture promotes things like consumerism, instant gratification, wealth,

Chapter 11

spending, indulgence, pleasure, sex, alcohol, escape, individualism, entitlement, and selfishness.

If you look deeper, you might find some positive things like teamwork, volunteering, and helping others, but these aren't as prominent as the rest. The reality is that our current culture cares more about what's trending than loving our neighbor. People tend to care more about getting the next best piece of technology than giving sacrificially to help the community.

Sadly, our culture has lost its moral center, truth is up for grabs, and if you don't tolerate everything, you are considered prejudiced or narrow-minded. Friends, the world is wrong. Our worldly culture has twisted things upside down and backward. The world has become a dangerous concoction of misguided values, mismatched philosophies, and forgotten beliefs. Our culture has exchanged the truth of God for lies. Many people have built their lives on the shifting sands of the temporary instead of pursuing what is eternal.

In contrast, Jesus gives us a great example of how to build our lives on a strong foundation by putting His words into practice in our lives.

> *Therefore everyone who hears these words of mine and puts them into practice is like a wise man who built his house on the rock. The rain came down, the streams rose, and the winds blew and beat against that house; yet it did not fall, because it had its foundation on the rock. But everyone who hears these words of mine and does not put them into practice is like a foolish man who built his house on sand. The rain came down, the streams rose, and the winds blew and beat against that house, and it fell with a great crash. (Matthew 7:24-27, NIV)*

Leading well means building our lives on the firm foundation of God's Word and putting His principles into practice in our daily lives. Faith-based leaders resist the urge to build their lives on the things that the culture values and seek to build their lives and their leadership on the things that God values.

WORLDLY VALUES:
Wrong Thinking

Have you ever been told you did something wrong? I remember when I was in first grade when Mrs. Magowen pulled me into the hallway to tell me I had done the coloring assignment wrong. I was confused because I carefully colored the Christmas tree design with my green crayons and stayed inside the lines. I followed her instructions to color it before I cut it out and glued it together. She then explained that the entire worksheet was a Christmas tree and that I had only colored the tinsel on the tree and not the tree itself. She was mad because she thought I ignored her directions. I was sad because I thought I did it right, but my thinking was wrong. I didn't realize the whole worksheet was a tree.

It might seem like a silly story, but many people have been chasing the things that the world values and don't realize that their thinking is wrong. What the world values isn't worth chasing. Things like popularity, status, power, achievement, possessions, beauty, fashion, and money do not last and do not satisfy the longings in our hearts. Sadly, we end up defining ourselves by these things, and our identity gets wrapped up in them. When this stuff fades away and is gone, we are left broken and hurt because we believed they would satisfy us and sustain us. However, our lives were made for so much more. In an interview with "60 Minutes," NFL quarterback Tom Brady shares about winning and his elusive search for satisfaction: [4]

> ***Brady:*** *"Why do I have three Super Bowl rings and still think there is something greater out there for me? I mean maybe a lot of people would say 'Hey man, this is what it is: I reached my goal, my dream...' Me, I think... there's got to be more than this... This can't be what it's all cracked up to be. I mean, I've done it. I'm 27... what else is there for me?"*

Chapter 11

> ***Moderator:*** *"What's the answer?"*
>
> ***Brady:*** *"I wish I knew. I wish I knew."* [61]

While Brady has won more championship rings since then, his comments as a young quarterback raise important questions: Where do we find meaning, and why don't things satisfy us like we thought they would?

It is difficult to engage in any type of television, news, internet, entertainment, mobile device, or social media outlet without advertisements trying to sell you something. The thirst for more is unquenchable, and the quest to please ourselves is unending. Much of the world's culture promotes a consumeristic mindset and "me" centered thinking. The enemy has sold us the wrong values and most people have believed the lies. As a result, people have come to value the wrong things and think the wrong things about their lives and their pursuits.

People without faith and without God live in a dark place and do dark things. Let's look at how Paul describes the way people act when they are left to themselves.

> *Since they thought it foolish to acknowledge God, he abandoned them to their foolish thinking and let them do things that should never be done. Their lives became full of every kind of wickedness, sin, greed, hate, envy, murder, quarreling, deception, malicious behavior, and gossip. They are backstabbers, haters of God, insolent, proud, and boastful. They invent new ways of sinning, and they disobey their parents. They refuse to understand, break their promises, are heartless, and have no mercy. They know God's justice requires that those who do these things deserve to die, yet they do them anyway. Worse yet, they encourage others to do them, too. (Romans 1:28-32, NLT)*

Left unchecked, corrupt hearts breed more corruption. That's what happens when we pursue worldly values and embrace wrong thinking. Over time, they lead to lives of wickedness. We need God to transform the way we think and to rescue us from our own corruption. Check out this advice about how to combat the values and thinking of the world.

> *Don't copy the behavior and customs of this world, but let God transform you into a new person by changing the way you think. Then you will learn to know God's will for you, which is good and pleasing and perfect. (Romans 12:2, NLT)*

Leading well means adopting God's values and allowing Him to transform the way we think and view the world. Faith-based leadership identifies the wrong thinking in our culture and seeks to point people toward faith-based thinking and living. Faith-based leaders understand that people have been led astray by the false promises of the world and actively try to help people rebuild their lives and their identity on the things of God.

WORLDLY FOCUS:
Wrong Priorities

Do you ever struggle with how to spend your time? Maybe you start the day with a list of tasks in your mind that you need to do but wonder in what order you should do them. Do they all have to get done or can some things wait until later? If there are things that you don't want to do, it can become easy to procrastinate or avoid the tasks altogether. However, problems arise when we focus on the wrong things and don't make the most important things a priority first. While life can often feel like a giant balancing act, there are some basic healthy pursuits worth our time.

We all have varying degrees of responsibilities, but the enemy wants us to focus on the wrong things and distract us into spending our time in an exhausting pursuit of the wrong stuff. When things like pursuing God, growing in our faith, loving our families, investing in our friends, and helping those around us take a backseat in our lives, something is wrong. If we are not careful, we can quickly start

Chapter 11

skipping or bailing on things that are vital to our health and longevity. Satan loves when we trade the vital and eternal things for the temporary and mundane. Check out Jesus' words to us about chasing the things of this world.

> *And what do you benefit if you gain the whole world but lose your own soul? Is anything worth more than your soul? (Matthew 16:26, NLT)*
>
> *Seek the Kingdom of God above all else, and live righteously, and he will give you everything you need. (Matthew 6:33, NLT)*

If you are looking for some help in prioritizing your life, there is no shortage of books, systems, philosophies, and quick fixes. However, here's a checklist for what order to pursue things based on Scripture and my own personal opinion.

1. Love God: First
- **Reach Up**: to know and love God
- **Reach In**: to grow and mature in faith

2. Love People: Second
- **Reach Out**: to serve and love others
    - 2nd - Love Your Spouse (if married)
    - 3rd - Love Your Kids (if it applies)
    - 4th - Love Others (serve, be a light, make disciples)
    - 5th - Work, School, Chores, Responsibilities
    - 6th - Sports, Clubs, Hobbies, Recreation, Entertainment

Now, you may not agree with me, and that's okay. But Jesus made it very clear that loving God and loving people are the two greatest commands (Matthew 22:36-40). I would argue that too many people get their priorities flipped and shifted out of order. In most people's lives, loving God gets pushed down and work, school, recreation, and other priorities get moved to the top. Yes, these things are important, but they are not the *most* important. However, sometimes priorities overlap, and things are not as clear-cut as they seem. While loving God and loving people can go hand-in-hand at times, the key is to keep God first in your life and leadership.

The enemy is great at getting us to focus on the wrong priorities. Even leaders in ministry get their priorities flipped and put their ministry to others above their own time with God, their marriages, or their families. We all struggle to spend our lives and our time wisely. Be encouraged that you are not alone, but be challenged that we must guard our lives, time, focus, and leadership against the push to make the less important things too high of priorities and neglect the best things.

While we cannot see Satan and his forces, we can certainly see the effects that they have on our world. What wrong priorities do you see in our world? What happens when people focus on worldly things and develop the wrong priorities? Well, that happens frequently. Over time, people drift into darkness and dark behavior follows. There's a cascade effect: a wrong foundation leads to wrong thinking, which leads to wrong priorities and wrong behavior. Check out what Paul says to the Galatian church about what happens when we drift away from what's right.

> *When you follow the desires of your sinful nature, the results are very clear: sexual immorality, impurity, lustful pleasures, idolatry, sorcery, hostility, quarreling, jealousy, outbursts of anger, selfish ambition, dissension, division, envy, drunkenness, wild parties, and other sins like these. Let me tell you again, as I have before, that anyone living that sort of life will not inherit the Kingdom of God. (Galatians 5:19-21, NLT)*

Strangely, these Bible verses sound a lot like a recap of a nightly news feed, a weekend movie review, or an upcoming television show to stream. The things people struggled with a long time ago are the same things today. The enemy's effects on the world continue to persist across time. To combat these things, we need to shift our priorities and our focus. The Bible is very clear about where our focus should be:

Chapter 11

> *And let us run with perseverance the race marked out for us, fixing our eyes on Jesus, the pioneer and perfecter of faith. (Hebrews 12:1b-2a, NIV)*

Leading well means keeping our focus on Jesus and our priorities centered around the things of God. It's a daily struggle to be sure, as there are many things vying for our time and attention. Faith-based leaders regularly review their priorities and their focus. They take time to correct and shift their lives and leadership to love God and love people accordingly. Leading with faith means focusing on the eternal versus the temporary and taking a long view of things. In addition, faith-based leadership helps others identify wrong priorities and encourages them to focus on the right things as well.

WORLDLY MOTIVES:
Wrong Intentions

If we were to shine a light on your motives, what would we find? Hopefully, you are an honest person with honorable motives. However, it might depend on the circumstances or the topic at hand.

The enemy is really good at twisting our desires. If he can't get us to do the wrong things, sometimes he can get us to pursue the right things with the wrong motives. There is no shortage of selfish motives in the world, and people often do things with wrong or misguided intentions. Motives and intentions are internal matters of the heart that are not easily seen, discerned, or revealed. What drives us to do things isn't always apparent, and it takes a confident leader to look inside himself or herself.

Leading with the wrong intentions can be a dangerous thing. It leaves our leadership open to manipulation, self-serving agendas, and using people for our own gain. I've led with mixed motives before, and the problem is our personal goals can quickly end up being in conflict with what's best for the group. Our decision-making can become biased or slanted, and our attention becomes divided.

We live in a corrupt world that has been shaped by Satan, his forces, and humanity's own sin. The worldly environment in which we live and lead is a toxic one that tests our motives, intentions, and even our prayers.

> ...Yet you don't have what you want because you don't ask God for it. And even when you ask, you don't get it because your motives are all wrong—you want only what will give you pleasure. You adulterers! Don't you realize that friendship with the world makes you an enemy of God? I say it again: If you want to be a friend of the world, you make yourself an enemy of God. (James 4:2b-4, NLT)

Sometimes, worldly living can seem very attractive at first. Chasing the things of this world can seem like an okay thing to do, but it's not. Our culture tends to glamorize sin and downplay the consequences. Many of the things that our culture promotes are in direct contrast to the things God desires from us. Think about it for a moment: What kinds of things does our culture promote? What kinds of motives do people generally have? The Bible cautions us about how we live and urges us not to engage in a worldly lifestyle, but rather be a light in the darkness.

> Carefully determine what pleases the Lord. Take no part in the worthless deeds of evil and darkness; instead, expose them. It is shameful even to talk about the things that ungodly people do in secret. But their evil intentions will be exposed when the light shines on them... (Ephesians 5:10-13, NLT)

Leading well means asking God to search our hearts and purify our motives and intentions. Faith-based leaders seek to surrender their selfish motives to God and ask Him to help them lead with honorable intentions. Leading with faith requires a vigilant guarding of our hearts against the powerful flow of our culture.

Chapter 11

WORLDLY PACE:
Wrong Speed

Most fans of NASCAR and IndyCar racing are familiar with the purpose of a pace car. The pace car usually leads the field of racers in a warmup lap at the beginning of a race or comes out during a track incident during the race to reset the racers. While the pace car is out front, it regulates everyone's speed, and no one is allowed to pass it.

Setting the proper pace is also important in running a race. Long-distance runners must pace themselves to spread out their energy and speed throughout the race so that they don't peak too soon. This enables them to complete the race with a strong push to the finish line. Finding the right pace can be tricky and takes practice: too fast and you burn out, too slow and you won't win.

Pace also plays a key role in our lives and our leadership. What is your current life pace? How busy are you? How stressed are you? How many plates of responsibilities do you have spinning in the air that need your regular attention? How much can you cram into one week? Probably quite a lot, but at what cost?

Most of the world operates at a fast pace. Some South American and African cultures have a slower pace, but overall our world functions at lightning speed. Fast food, fast shipping, fast checkout, fast lanes, quick fixes, quick growth, instant communication, and instant gratification all define the speed of our cultural landscape. Our culture likes things fast, and people often pay Amazon extra to get their stuff even faster. Our culture is also great at keeping people busy. Companies, schools, churches, clubs, and teams pride themselves on how much they can cram into their schedules, and they are all fighting for people's limited time and attention.

The enemy loves to distract us by keeping us so busy and by keeping the pace so high that we don't take time for what's most important. Most of us don't have much margin, buffer, or rest in our lives. Our days, weeks, and calendars are so jam-packed with responsibilities and activities that we barely have time to eat, sleep, or renew ourselves. The problem is that the world doesn't value slow-and-steady hard work, rest, renewal, pausing, or any kind of buffer in our lives. Sadly, we can quickly start skipping things like family meals, church, time with God, personal renewal, and sleep. We can get so tired and worn out from working long hours that we drop the ball on our responsibilities, chores, homework, and relationships because we are so fried.

Setting a healthy pace for yourself and those you lead is counter-cultural, but it is much needed. Slow down the machine and take some time to evaluate what a healthy pace looks like for your leadership context. Find out what your group or team needs and re-adjust your pace. In general, what does a healthy pace look like? Well, God encourages us to press "pause" at least once a week.

> *Remember to observe the Sabbath day by keeping it holy. You have six days each week for your ordinary work, but the seventh day is a Sabbath day of rest dedicated to the LORD your God. (Exodus 20:8-10a, NLT)*

> *Be still, and know that I am God! I will be honored by every nation. I will be honored throughout the world. (Psalm 46:10, NLT)*

Unfortunately, our lives and our leadership end up being evaluated on our productivity (how much), efficiency (how fast), and accuracy (how correct) we can do things without regard for the health of the person. The pace and pressure of these things can push our lives in an unhealthy and stressful direction.

As a former university Professor of Biology and Stress Physiology, Dan shares a few insights about the impact of stress as it relates to the pace of our culture. Stress is a part of life, and up to a point, it can be beneficial. Stress can challenge us to better ourselves, but it can also hurt us. Most of the time, stress is a major distraction and harmful to the body especially when the pace gets hectic like it is in society today. In a typical stress response, the body turns on many systems to allow a better chance of survival in a life-threatening situation. The hormonal system accelerates cortisol and adrenaline to increase energy supply, heart rate, and heart pumping ability.

Chapter 11

Additionally, the brain accelerates the firing of neurons to respond faster and muscle strength increases, just to mention a few. These responses all help to fight or flee a life-threatening situation, but the problem is that most daily stress situations are not life-threatening. Over time, the repeated intensity of our triggered stress response can wear down the body. When this happens, daily fatigue quickly sets in and causes harmful effects on the body.

Some of the harmful effects of prolonged stress include high blood pressure, heart disease, heart attack, mental health issues, emotional distress, weight gain, and trouble sleeping. To complicate the issue, many people have poor coping mechanisms such as increased alcohol and tobacco use, substance abuse, overeating, undereating, craving salty or sweet foods, higher caffeine intake, overuse of energy drinks and energy boosters, self-harm, and addictive behaviors. All of these behaviors only mask our problems and don't actually deal with the stress. Instead, people need to pursue positive techniques like exercise, a healthy diet, talking to friends, listening to music, journaling, praying, sharing with a counselor, or slowing the pace.

If you are sick of the rat race, the crazy pace, and living your life on fast forward, then take a moment to breathe and find comfort in these words from Jesus:

> *Then Jesus said, "Come to me, all of you who are weary and carry heavy burdens, and I will give you rest. Take my yoke upon you. Let me teach you, because I am humble and gentle at heart, and you will find rest for your souls. For my yoke is easy to bear, and the burden I give you is light." (Matthew 11:28-30, NLT)*

After pastoring American high school students for over 25 years, I have learned that some of their biggest complaints about life are how busy, tired, and stressed out they are. The pressure and pace of life weighed heavily on them. In fact, some nights when we would meet, I would just let them kick back, rest, chill, hangout, and catch their breath for a bit. We would dial back our program, simplify things, have an extended time of sharing, and reset our pace to better serve our students- and they loved it.

Leading well means slowing the hustle and bustle of life long enough to take inventory of our current pace and re-adjust our speed. Maybe it's too fast or maybe it's too slow. Invite some trusted friends to give you input on the pace of your life and leadership. Faith-based leaders are aware of Satan's tactics and fight against the pace of the culture to create space and develop a pace that honors God. Does the pace of your leadership exhaust or frustrate those you lead? How could a healthier pace enhance your leadership and your team's longevity?

THE RUB:
Leading in an Uncooperative World

How does infusing faith into our leadership affect our view of the environment in which we lead? Faith reevaluates our leadership landscape as we seek to lead others in a fallen world in three key ways.

First, we look inward. With a little self-evaluation, we can ask ourselves some enlightening questions: How does the toxic environment of our worldly culture affect our leadership? In what ways has the enemy influenced your foundation, thinking, priorities, motives, and pace? What would it take to combat the enemy's influence on those areas and tighten up your defenses against his attacks on your life and leadership?

Second, we look outward. How does the worldly environment and culture affect the people we lead? Why is the world so uncooperative and resistant to faith-based leadership? What makes leading in a fallen world so hard? With a little team evaluation, we can ask some enlightening questions: How is the current worldly culture affecting your company, team, church, school, or family? In what ways has the enemy influenced the foundation, thinking, priorities, motives, and pace of the people you lead?

Third, we become counter-cultural. If this were a boxing match, the proper response to our opponent's punch is a blocking move followed by a counterpunch. Faith-based leaders learn to counter the cultural norms with faith-based alternatives. We counter a wrong foundation with helping people build their lives on Christ. We counter wrong thinking with the truth and teachings of the Bible. We counter wrong priorities by developing an eternal perspective and refocusing on what really matters. We counter wrong intentions and motives with an honest look inside by examining our hearts. We counter the wrong speed and pace by pausing to check our current speed, change gears, and choose a healthier pace.

> **FROM THE TRENCHES**
> **WHAT DOES IT TAKE TO LEAD WELL IN YOUR LEADERSHIP CONTEXT?**
>
> "FIRST, WHILE IT'S IMPORTANT TO SEEK INPUT FROM TRUSTED ADVISORS, YOU CAN'T LEAD WELL BY COMMITTEE. SECOND, YOU CAN'T EXPECT THOSE YOU ARE LEADING TO WORK HARDER THAN YOU DO. YOU MUST ESTABLISH AND MAINTAIN THE WORK ETHIC YOU DESIRE FOR YOUR TEAM BY THE EXAMPLE THAT YOU LIVE."
>
> -STEVE FRANCIS
> OWNER AT WELLSPRING BUILDERS,
> COMMERCIAL CONSTRUCTION [62]

PUTTING IT INTO PRACTICE

Before you move on, think about, discuss, and apply the following questions as they relate to your leadership within your company, team, church, school, or family.

Leadership Thoughts

1. What key points stick out to you from this chapter and why?
2. What happens when people have the wrong foundation, thinking, priorities, motives, and pace?
3. How does infusing faith into your leadership affect your view of the environment in which you lead?
4. Look inward: How has the enemy influenced your foundation, thinking, priorities, motives, and pace; what can you do to combat the enemy and tighten your defenses?
5. Look outward: How is the current worldly culture affecting your company, team, church, school, or family, and why does it make it hard to lead well?
6. Become counter-cultural: What cultural norms do you and your group need to counter with faith-based alternatives?

CHAPTER 12
THE ENEMY WITHIN
Featured Leader: Adam

Many people don't realize that there is a hidden enemy deep within us that corrupts our lives and our leadership. There is an ugly selfishness that hides beneath the surface and taints our motives, drives our hearts, shapes our thinking, and pushes our behavior in the wrong direction. We don't like to admit it, but in our honest moments alone with our hearts, we know there is something off and something is deeply wrong inside of us. There are desires we don't want to talk about, thoughts that we are ashamed of, and secret behaviors that we hope no one finds out. Don't worry; you're not crazy. There is a reason for all of that, and it started a long time ago with a leader named Adam.

ADAM'S CURSE

There are helpful but unsettling leadership principles that we can learn from the life of Adam and how his corrupt nature was passed along to us. We can see this corruption through his <u>choices and consequences</u>, our <u>corrupt nature</u>, our <u>corrupt hearts</u>, our <u>corrupt minds</u>, and our <u>corrupt behaviors</u>.

ADAM'S CURSE

- **Choices and Consequences**
  (Genesis 2:15-17, 3:6, Galatians 6:7-8)
- **Corrupt Nature**
  (Romans 5:12, 18-19)
- **Corrupt Heart**
  (Mark 7:21-23, Jeremiah 17:9)
- **Corrupt Mind**
  (Romans 8:5-8)
- **Corrupt Behavior**
  (Galatians 5:19-21)

CORRUPTION

amplifyministries.org

CHOICES AND CONSEQUENCES

Life is full of choices: fun choices, tough choices, good choices, bad choices, and everything in between. Having the ability to choose is one of the great things about being human. Which of these fun choices would you rather pick: Chocolate or vanilla? Cake or pie? American muscle cars or European exotics? New shoes or a new purse? Mountains or the beach? One player or four players? Dark roast coffee or caramel mocha frappuccino?

Here are some tougher choices: Saving or spending? Kindness or rudeness? Forgiveness or bitterness? Self-centered or others-centered? Generosity or greed? Instant gratification or delayed reward? Obedience or disobedience? The choices are endless, but with each choice we make there are positive or negative consequences. Some are mild, and some have a heavy impact.

Adam was the father of humanity. He was given free will, guidelines, and the ability to make his own choices, and so was his wife, Eve. As the first humans, God created them this way and gave them freedom to make their own decisions. With that freedom came the option to follow God in obedience or to disobey Him and face the

Chapter 12

consequences. As representatives of the entire human race, Adam and Eve's choices had a massive impact on all the people to come.

> *The LORD God placed the man in the Garden of Eden to tend and watch over it. But the LORD God warned him, "You may freely eat the fruit of every tree in the garden— except the tree of the knowledge of good and evil. If you eat its fruit, you are sure to die." (Genesis 2:15-17, NLT)*

> *When the woman saw that the fruit of the tree was good for food and pleasing to the eye, and also desirable for gaining wisdom, she took some and ate it. She also gave some to her husband, who was with her, and he ate it. (Genesis 3:6, NIV)*

Adam chose poorly. Adam and Eve gave into temptation, ate the forbidden fruit, and broke God's command. Unfortunately, humans would never be the same after that. Their sin marked the fall of humanity, and the consequences of their choices would ripple throughout history. Like it or not, we all must live with the devastating results of their actions. Our nature would be forever changed and humanity's right relationship with God was now broken.

Even so, we are all given free will to choose good or evil. Each day is full of choices and consequences. We have the choice to follow God or to follow our own sinful desires. The Bible makes it clear that we are free to live for ourselves or to live to please the Lord. We can follow the light, or we can live in darkness. Which path we choose will not only affect our character and our leadership, but also our eternal destiny. How you live your life is up to you but be warned... if you live in darkness and plant bad seeds in the soil of your life, then bad things will grow. However, if you live in the light and plant good seeds, then good things will grow. Choose wisely because we reap what we sow.

> *Don't be misled—you cannot mock the justice of God. You will always harvest what you plant. Those who live only to satisfy their own sinful nature will harvest*

> *decay and death from that sinful nature. But those who live to please the Spirit will harvest everlasting life from the Spirit. (Galatians 6:7-8, NLT)*

Faith-based leaders choose to live in the light and work diligently to plant good seeds in the soil of their lives and in their leadership. They resist temptation and seek wisdom. Leading well involves weighing the options and potential consequences and making wise choices in the best interest of the people you are leading. In the sci-fi television series "Andromeda," Captain Dylan Hunt describes good leadership this way: *"Figure out what the people really need and then figure out the best and safest way to get it for them. From there, everything else follows."* [63]

CORRUPT NATURE

Adam chose to disobey God and sin entered the world. As a result, Adam and Eve were cursed, banished from the Garden of Eden, and a sinful nature was passed on to all of humanity. From then on, all people would bear the curse as well.

> *When Adam sinned, sin entered the world. Adam's sin brought death, so death spread to everyone, for everyone sinned. (Romans 5:12, NLT)*

What does it mean that we all have a sinful or corrupt nature? Well, it means that sin has corrupted God's original design for us. The corruption of sin penetrates all aspects of our being: heart, mind, and behavior. The way we feel, think, and act is deeply affected by our sinful desires. Our sinful nature is the enemy within us, and it seeks to undermine and destroy our leadership. Not everyone recognizes this or agrees with it, but it's true. There is corruption within all of us.

Think of it this way—sin is a lot like salt. Salt is corrosive to metal just like sin is corrosive to our lives. Growing up in the Midwest, we had snowy winters. Snow is fun, but snowy roads meant the city would send out the salt trucks. Salt on the roads meant rust on your

Chapter 12

cars. Like salt eats away metal and creates rust, a sinful nature eats away at our hearts and rusts out our lives.

What are the results and consequences of a corrupt nature? Because we all have inherited a corrupt nature, life is now harder, and leadership is harder. We constantly live with an internal battle to live right or wrong and to lead well or not. We must battle our own sinful nature, making our leadership and the quest to lead well much more difficult. Not only that, but we also must battle other people's sinful natures.

However, there is good news. In Christ, we can have access to a new nature. When we put our faith in Jesus, we are given a new life and new nature in Christ.

> *Yes, Adam's one sin brings condemnation for everyone, but Christ's one act of righteousness brings a right relationship with God and new life for everyone. Because one person disobeyed God, many became sinners. But because one other person obeyed God, many will be made righteous. (Romans 5:18-19, NLT)*

We can have victory over our sinful nature, but it's not easy. I'll explain more about how we can do that later in the next chapter. For now, it is a daily struggle between our old nature and our new one. Leading well means that each of us must battle against sin and corruption within ourselves.

CORRUPT HEART

Corruption can be found almost anywhere: politics, businesses, police departments, judicial systems, insurance companies, churches, athletic competitions, city councils, and educational institutions. Unfortunately, cheaters, hackers, scammers, and secret agendas are abundant in our culture.

From a corrupt nature comes a corrupt heart which leads to corrupt thinking and corrupt actions. Check out what the Bible has to say about our hearts and the enemy within...

> *For from within, out of a person's heart, come evil thoughts, sexual immorality, theft, murder, adultery, greed, wickedness, deceit, lustful desires, envy, slander, pride, and foolishness. All these vile things come from within; they are what defile you." (Mark 7:21-23, NLT)*

> *The human heart is the most deceitful of all things, and desperately wicked. Who really knows how bad it is? (Jeremiah 17:9 NLT)*

Leading well requires a careful evaluation of our own hearts and sinful desires on a regular basis. It is a daily challenge to keep our sinful nature and corrupt hearts in check. Because the enemy within us seeks to destroy our leadership, ruin our credibility, and sabotage our relationships, it is vital to protect ourselves and our leadership from corruption. We must identify our weaknesses and be alert to tempting situations.

> *Temptation comes from our own desires, which entice us and drag us away. These desires give birth to sinful actions. And when sin is allowed to grow, it gives birth to death. (James 1:14-15, NLT)*

While good things can come out of our hearts sometimes, leading well recognizes our human tendency to go astray and takes steps to guard against the temptations we face. Faith-based leadership confesses the corruption in our hearts and asks God to purify our lives and protect our leadership from corruption.

CORRUPT MIND

We all wrestle with corrupt thoughts from time to time. It is easy to allow our minds to wander and end up thinking some wild thoughts. Our society, culture, and the media are great at twisting the meaning, manipulating our thinking, hiding the truth, and getting us to believe all sorts of things. People are frequently bombarded with

Chapter 12

corrupt thoughts and distorted views. With so many things trying to influence us, it can be a real struggle to push the noise aside and hold on to what's right and true. However, the real struggle for our mind is not external, but internal. The real battle is inside our heads.

> *Those who are dominated by the sinful nature think about sinful things, but those who are controlled by the Holy Spirit think about things that please the Spirit. So letting your sinful nature control your mind leads to death. But letting the Spirit control your mind leads to life and peace. For the sinful nature is always hostile to God. It never did obey God's laws, and it never will. That's why those who are still under the control of their sinful nature can never please God. (Romans 8:5-8, NLT)*

Out of a corrupt heart comes a corrupt mind, and what we allow ourselves to think about eventually comes out in our behavior. Leading well means taking action against our corrupt thoughts and feeding our minds biblical truth and anchoring our thinking in sound teaching and solid principles. It takes a disciplined and renewed mind to lead well.

> *Do not conform to the pattern of this world, but be transformed by the renewing of your mind. (Romans 12:2a, NIV)*

Faith-based leadership recognizes our corrupt minds and engages in the daily battle to renew our thinking, to corral our wayward thoughts, and to purify our minds. The pull of sinful thoughts is powerful, and it takes a transformed life and mind to resist, stand firm, and lead well.

CORRUPT BEHAVIOR

We are all broken people, and we act badly at times. In a moment of frustration, it can be easy to lash out in some unholy ways.

It is common to yell and scream, cuss and swear, punch and kick, or to mock and insult people who offend and annoy us. It can be hard to show restraint in the heat of the moment, and often our poor behavior can get us into a heap of trouble.

No one has to teach kids how to be mean or throw fits; it's in their nature, and it's in ours too. Corrupt and sinful behaviors are the result of a corrupt nature. It's not pretty, but sinful people sin. While our corrupt behavior is just a symptom of a corrupt heart and mind, it's the ugliest and messiest part of our corruption because it's what people see. This outward manifestation of our inward corruption takes on many forms...

> *When you follow the desires of your sinful nature, the results are very clear: sexual immorality, impurity, lustful pleasures, idolatry, sorcery, hostility, quarreling, jealousy, outbursts of anger, selfish ambition, dissension, division, envy, drunkenness, wild parties, and other sins like these... (Galatians 5:19-21a, NLT)*

No one likes to admit it, but we do stupid, mean, and selfish stuff. We sin, mess up, hurt people, act inappropriately, and our behavior can be downright nasty and unacceptable. Welcome to being human! However, we were made for so much more. Leading well means acting well, and that takes a lifetime of self-control, personal discipline, lots of apologies, making better choices, and a resilient faith. See if you can relate to how Paul describes his own struggle with his sinful nature and behavior:

> *And I know that nothing good lives in me, that is, in my sinful nature. I want to do what is right, but I can't. I want to do what is good, but I don't. I don't want to do what is wrong, but I do it anyway. But if I do what I don't want to do, I am not really the one doing wrong; it is sin living in me that does it. I have discovered this principle of life—that when I want to*

do what is right, I inevitably do what is wrong. (Romans 7:18-21, NLT)

Faith-based leaders fight the urge to behave badly and seek to honor God and others with their actions. Leading well means acknowledging our weaknesses and tendency toward corrupt behavior and challenging ourselves and others to a higher standard of personal conduct.

THE RUB: The Inner Battle

How does infusing faith into our leadership affect how we view the nature of people? Faith identifies a hidden enemy within us and highlights the inner battle that we all must face. To lead well, we must battle the enemy within ourselves and learn how to deal with the enemy within other people.

The Enemy Within Us: Leading Ourselves

It's a leadership fact, leaders are flawed. Even the best leaders have flaws, shortcomings, and weaknesses. So, how do we lead ourselves well in light of this truth? It starts with admitting that we are not perfect, acknowledging our own corrupt nature, and knowing our weak spots. We need to surrender to God and ask Him for help with our leadership. We need trusted friends to help us examine our own shortcomings, take measures to correct or curb these issues, and surround ourselves with people that complement our leadership gaps.

In the next chapter, I will talk in detail about how we can have victory over the enemies to faith-based leadership and give you a game plan for living a life of victory.

The Enemy Within Them: Leading Fallen People

It's a leadership fact, people are flawed. We lead in a world full of flawed, corrupted, and fallen people. So how do we lead fallen people and how does that affect our leadership? Well, for starters fallen people usually *resist* good leadership. They can be stubborn, sinful, and difficult to lead. Recognizing that the people we are leading have a corrupt nature will help us have a stronger sense of compassion and understanding toward them. Or if we choose to deny or overlook their corrupt hearts and minds, it will frustrate us, anger us, and exhaust us repeatedly until we have no desire to lead them anymore.

LEADERSHIP SPOTLIGHT: THE REALITY OF LEADING

People will be late to meetings, drop the ball, miss the goal, forget the report, offend the client, talk behind our backs, break promises, and disappoint us. Because of that, leading fallen people requires a generous amount of love, care, and forgiveness. Despite their shortcomings, people can also hit the mark, win the game, sacrifice for the team, develop character, strengthen their resolve, work overtime, overcome obstacles, rise above the competition, and come through for us in big ways with the proper balance of leadership, inspiration, correction, understanding, and support.

Remember the people and teams you lead are only human, so try not to let corrupt behavior surprise you. Sinful people sin. You don't have to accept it but expect it from time to time. They are on a journey just like you. Offer correction; give guidance; and forgive often. Challenge them to be better; lead by example; and love them regardless.

Chapter 12

> **FROM THE TRENCHES**
> **WHAT DOES IT TAKE TO LEAD WELL IN YOUR LEADERSHIP CONTEXT?**
>
> "Leadership is like a string. You can't push it forward from the back or it crumbles. You have to pull it from the front. You have to lead by example. Show them how to do it and why. Then they will remember how it's done."
>
> -Anni Orefice
> Hotel and Restaurant Specialist, Germany [64]

PUTTING IT INTO PRACTICE

Before you move on, think about, discuss, and apply the following questions as they relate to your leadership within your company, team, church, school, or family.

Leadership Thoughts

1. What key points stick out to you from this chapter and why?
2. How does infusing faith into your leadership affect how you view the nature of people?
3. How does having to battle with your own fallen nature affect how you lead?
4. How does having to deal with other people's fallen nature affect how you lead them?
5. What roles do compassion, grace, forgiveness, and correction play in leading corrupt people in a corrupt world?
6. What can you do to guard your life and your leadership from sin and corruption?

CHAPTER 13
VICTORY OVER THE ENEMY
Featured Leader: You

OUR VICTORY

We can learn amazing and freeing leadership principles from a life of faith and how we can have victory over the enemy of our faith and the enemy within us. We can see this path to victory through <u>surrender to God</u>, as we <u>start trusting</u>, as we <u>stop sinning</u>, as we learn to <u>stand firm</u>, and as we <u>seek accountability</u> from trusted friends.

OUR VICTORY

❶ **Surrender to God**
(Psalm 51: 1-4a, 1 John 1:8-9)

❷ **Start Trusting**
(Proverbs 3:5-6, Psalm 25:4-5)

❸ **Stop Sinning**
(Colossians 3:5-10)

❹ **Stand Firm**
(1 Corinthians 16:13-14, 1 Peter 5:8-9)

❺ **Seek Accountability**
(Galatians 6:1-2)

FAITH

amplifyministries.org

SURRENDER TO GOD

Usually, the road to recovery starts with admitting you need help. If you are familiar with addiction and recovery groups it might go something like this: *"My name is Larry, and I am a sinful person."* The group waves and responds: *"Hi, Larry!"* I continue: *"I know that I have a corrupt nature, and I need help."* The group applauds and responds: *"Welcome to the Sinful Person Recovery Group! You have taken the first step on the road to a better life and better leadership."* This illustration might seem a bit silly, but there is an important truth about how we can overcome the corruption within us and lead a life of victory. It begins with an honest look inside ourselves and a willingness to surrender.

Since we have a corrupt nature that infiltrates our hearts, minds, and behaviors, what do we do? The solution to a corrupt nature is a new nature. The solution to a corrupt heart is a spiritual heart transplant. The solution to a corrupt mind is a renewed mind. The solution to corrupt behavior is a completely transformed life. None of these things can be done on our own. God is the only one who can help us, and it starts with surrendering our hearts, minds, and lives to Him.

> *Have mercy on me, O God, because of your unfailing love. Because of your great compassion, blot out the stain of my sins. Wash me clean from my guilt. Purify me from my sin. For I recognize my rebellion; it haunts me day and night. Against you, and you alone, have I sinned; I have done what is evil in your sight. (Psalm 51:1-4a, NLT)*

> *If we claim we have no sin, we are only fooling ourselves and not living in the truth. But if we confess our sins to him, he is faithful and just to forgive us our sins and to cleanse us from all wickedness. (1 John 1:8-9, NLT)*

While the first step in fighting a corrupt nature is our initial confession of sins and surrender of our lives to Christ. There is also an

Chapter 13

ongoing component. As followers of God, we continue to do battle against our old nature through a daily surrender to Christ.

Faith-based leadership continually surrenders our hearts, minds, and behaviors to God and asks him to forgive us, purify us, and protect us. Here's an example of how to do that:

Leadership Prayer of Surrender

"Jesus, help me lead well today. I surrender my life and my leadership to you. Forgive my sinfulness and purify my motives and desires. Help me serve, love, and value the people I am leading. Bless my leadership and may it honor you. Please, protect me from all the enemies of my leadership both inside of me and outside of me. Grant me victory in the name of Jesus. Amen."

START TRUSTING

Having victory over the enemy of our faith and the enemy within us involves trusting ourselves less and trusting God more. Our human wisdom, understanding, and perspective can be useful, but it has its limits. Because we lack completeness in these areas and are vulnerable to corruption, it is vital to our leadership that we continually trust and rely on God.

> *Trust in the LORD with all your heart; do not depend on your own understanding. Seek his will in all you do, and he will show you which path to take. (Proverbs 3:5-6, NLT)*

> *Show me the right path, O LORD; point out the road for me to follow. Lead me by your truth and teach me, for you are the God who saves me. All day long I put my hope in you. (Psalm 25:4-5, NLT)*

Faith-based leaders don't just trust God occasionally; they live lives that are regularly dependent on Him. Asking God for help and guidance becomes a lifelong habit and empowers us to lead well. Faith-based leaders have a teachable spirit and are open to what God is trying to accomplish in us and through us. Leading well means trusting God to lead us as we lead our families, companies, churches, schools, and teams.

Leadership Prayer of Trust

"God, I put my trust in you today. Help me lead well by relying on your wisdom and direction. I recognize the limits of my own wisdom and understanding, and I seek your guidance. I lift all my plans and decisions up to you. Show me which paths to take. Please, lead me as I lead others, and bless my leadership. In the name of Jesus, I pray. Amen."

STOP SINNING

Having victory over the enemies to our leadership takes hard work, perseverance, and self-control. Fighting our corrupt nature and the corruption of the world involves a righteous determination to resist temptation. It is hard to lead well if we are living in sin. Recognizing our poor thoughts and behaviors, confessing them to God, and then turning away from those things becomes an essential part of having personal and professional victory.

> *So put to death the sinful, earthly things lurking within you. Have nothing to do with sexual immorality, impurity, lust, and evil desires. Don't be greedy, for a greedy person is an idolater, worshiping the things of this world. Because of these sins, the anger of God is coming. You used to do these things when your life was still part of this world. But now is the time to get rid of anger, rage, malicious behavior, slander, and dirty language. Don't lie to each other, for you have stripped off your old sinful nature and all its wicked deeds. Put on your new nature, and be renewed as you learn to know your Creator and become like him. (Colossians 3:5-10, NLT)*

Chapter 13

The goal is to sin less and to become more and more like Christ in our attitudes, thoughts, and actions. Spiritual growth is a life-long journey, and we are all at different places along the path. Choosing right living and avoiding sin is part of that process. As we pursue moral growth, we develop and improve personally. This personal development strengthens our character and enhances our leadership.

> *Those who belong to Christ Jesus have nailed the passions and desires of their sinful nature to his cross and crucified them there. Since we are living by the Spirit, let us follow the Spirit's leading in every part of our lives. (Galatians 5:24-25, NLT)*

Stopping the sin in our lives and choosing to live for God is a daily struggle and a lifelong process. We constantly need Christ's help and the strength of God's Spirit to do it. However, we are not trying to earn God's favor with the right behavior. We can't. Additionally, the goal is not to live a perfect life. We can't do that either. That's why Christ died for our sins. Leading well means striving to live honorably, sin less, and lean hard on God's grace and forgiveness when we make mistakes.

Leadership Prayer of Confession

"Jesus, help me stop sinning and lead a life that honors you. I confess that I think and act in ways that are sinful and dishonorable. Please, forgive me for my mistakes and help me live better. Bless my leadership and help me lead well by resisting temptation and choosing to avoid sinful things. Purify my heart, mind, body, and actions, and help me become more like you. I pray in your name. Amen."

STAND FIRM

Like a lighthouse stands firm as a guardian of light and protects ships from danger, our faith can help us stand firm against the dangers of the world and protect our leadership from running aground. Leadership is dangerous and faith-based leadership is especially dangerous because Satan does not want us to lead well. Faith-based leaders are under ongoing spiritual attack and must learn to stand firm against the forces of darkness that seek to shipwreck our lives and destroy our leadership effectiveness.

> *Be on guard. Stand firm in the faith. Be courageous. Be strong. And do everything with love." (1 Corinthians 16:13-14, NLT)*

> *Stay alert! Watch out for your great enemy, the devil. He prowls around like a roaring lion, looking for someone to devour. Stand firm against him, and be strong in your faith. (1 Peter 5:8-9a, NLT)*

If you are trying to infuse faith into your leadership like we are recommending, then be prepared. The devil wants to ruin your family, company, school, church, and teams. So, take these words to heart. Be on guard, hold up the shield of your faith, stand your ground, and resist the enemy. It might sound overly dramatic or like something from *The Lord of the Rings* movies, but it's not. The forces of darkness and light are real. Whether we recognize them or not, we feel their effects on us all the time. The desire to do good must be encouraged and the strong pull to do evil must be resisted. Leading well means standing firm in our faith and holding fast to the Word of God.

> *Therefore, put on every piece of God's armor so you will be able to resist the enemy in the time of evil. Then after the battle you will still be standing firm. (Ephesians 6:13)*

> *Submit yourselves, then, to God. Resist the devil, and he will flee from you. Come near to God and he will come near to you. (James 4:7-8a, NIV)*

It can be difficult to stand firm in the face of challenging circumstances, and our faith is often tested beyond what feels reasonable. The ups and downs of life and leadership can be brutal.

Chapter 13

Life can quickly become stressful, overwhelming, and hard to handle. During these times it is essential to draw near to God, anchor ourselves to Him, clothe ourselves in God's armor, and keep resisting the worry, fear, doubt, and temptations that plague us.

Leadership Prayer of Strength

"Lord, help me stand firm in my faith and cling to the hope I have in you. Please give me the strength and endurance that I need to lead well today. I come near to you and resist the enemy. Help me be strong and courageous and give me a steady heart to face whatever the day holds. Help me be a light for you and for the people I lead. I pray in the name of Jesus. Amen."

SEEK ACCOUNTABILITY

It is not easy to live a life of faith and to lead well on your own. It takes good people in your life who care about your health and well-being to help you keep your life, faith, and leadership on track. Leaning on trusted friends and colleagues can make a big difference in our battle against the corruption within us and keep us in leadership for a long time. Having a few faith-based friendships with people who know your weaknesses, short-comings, and struggles can make all the difference between personal failure and personal victory. Inviting them to hold you accountable to high standards of moral conduct, issues of faith, and professional ethics can strengthen your character and enhance your leadership over the long term.

> *Dear brothers and sisters, if another believer is overcome by some sin, you who are godly should gently and humbly help that person back onto the right path. And be careful not to fall into the same temptation yourself. Share each other's burdens, and in this way obey the law of Christ. (Galatians 6:1-2, NLT)*
>
> *Two are better than one, because they have a good return for their labor: If either of them falls down, one*

can help the other up. But pity anyone who falls and has no one to help them up. (Ecclesiastes 4:9-10, NIV)

Personally, my close friends have played a pivotal role in my leadership journey. They have helped me fight the sinful corruption in my own heart. They have kept me on track when I was tempted to go astray. They have been a sounding board when I needed advice. They have been an anchor and an encouragement when my faith was weak. They have helped me become a better person, husband, father, and leader. These types of friends are rare and being accountable to them in my personal and professional life has made me a better man. I encourage you to find and build some accountability into your life and take a risk by opening up with some trusted people to better yourself.

Leadership Prayer of Accountability

"God, help me seek accountability in my life. Please provide trusted friends to help me follow you and lead well. Bring the right people into my life to help strengthen my faith, help me resist sin, and become a better person. Help me be honest about my struggles, confess when I make mistakes, and set goals to improve myself. Help me lead well today by keeping my life and heart on the right path. In Jesus name, Amen."

THE WIN: Personal Victory

How does infusing faith into our leadership affect how we pursue victory in our personal lives? Faith redefines our ability to overcome and gives us a new set of tools to achieve personal victory. By surrendering to God, trusting Him, resisting sin, standing firm in our faith, and seeking accountability, we can have victory over the unique enemies of faith-based leadership *(Satan and sin)*.

While most leaders don't recognize these enemies, even traditional leadership models acknowledge human nature and the need to confront our dark side.[65] While there are many common enemies to all leadership that lurk within us like: greed, envy, lust, power, control, ambition, pride, ego, and selfishness. Faith-based leadership has the ability to combat these things at the source by

Chapter 13

confessing our corrupt nature. Through our faith, we can address the problem of corruption within our own hearts, tackle it with the power of God, and find victory over the darkness.

While the struggle to lead well is ongoing, many faith-based leaders have found true and lasting victory over the enemy within and the enemy of our faith. It is possible to live a life of victory and lead victoriously. It takes a continual surrender to God, a disciplined mind and body, an understanding of God's Word, a reliance on Christ's strength in us, and a fair amount of leaning on good friends.

Leadership Prayer of Victory

"Jesus, give me victory over the sin in my life and over my sinful nature. Protect me from the power and influence of Satan and help me stand firm in my faith. Help me lead well today by surrendering to you, trusting your leading in my life, and being accountable to my close friends. Please, grant me personal victory over the darkness and help me lead victoriously. I pray in your name. Amen."

LEADERSHIP REBORN

FROM THE TRENCHES
What does it take to lead well in your leadership context?

"My victory starts with the thought, 'My day is His; my life is His.' I have Christ's resurrection power in me. From that, I take my thoughts and feelings captive, and live in the truth. I choose to focus on the good and not the bad. I fight the battle by trying to stay humble and kind, lean on others, and worship a lot. I push myself with positive self-talk to do more and to keep moving forward."

-Julie Francis
Nurse Practitioner [66]

Chapter 13

SECTION SUMMARY

Great job completing this heavy section on the enemies to faith-based leadership and how we can overcome them. We covered some tough topics! Hopefully, you gained some important insights into the enemy's tactics, your own internal battles, and how to take positive steps toward victory. Here's what is coming up last in part four: The Art of Leading Well. We'll review what we have covered and pull all the leadership concepts together.

PUTTING IT INTO PRACTICE

Before you move on, think about, discuss, and apply the following questions as they relate to your leadership within your company, team, church, school, or family.

Leadership Thoughts

1. What key points stick out to you from this chapter and why?
2. How does gaining victory in our personal lives affect our leadership effectiveness?
3. How does infusing faith into our leadership affect how we pursue victory in our personal lives?
4. How has your faith in God helped you have personal victory in your life?
5. What are some practical steps you can take this month to resist a specific sin, to stand firm in your faith, and to ask a friend to help keep you on track?
6. If you haven't yet, take some time to pray the various leadership prayers from this chapter. Which leadership prayer impacted you the most and why?

PART 4

LEADING WITH FAITH

CHAPTER 14

THE ART OF LEADING WELL

Congrats! You made it to the last chapter. Thanks for investing in your own leadership development and persevering in your leadership and faith journey. We have covered a lot of leadership ground over the course of this book. Hopefully, you have been able to learn, grow, and apply some of the leadership principles that we have discussed.

However, putting all these leadership concepts into practice all the time can seem like an overwhelming task. It takes time and experience to lead well, and chances are you can't do it all at once. So, don't try to do it all right away. This chapter is a summary of all the leaders, main points, and leadership principles that we have talked about. It is designed to help you remember what we have covered, to help you break the book down into smaller manageable parts, and to help you pick areas to focus on.

The world is full of leaders, and a lot of people can lead, but not everyone leads well. Actually, most people don't lead well. Leading well is an art. It is a combination of learned leadership skills, natural talent, hard work, experience, God-given ability, personal development, and allowing your faith to infuse all aspects of how you lead others. We believe that the art of leading well requires more than traditional leadership models and skills, it requires faith in God. With the right foundation in place, leading well becomes very possible.

This entire book is dedicated to the art of leading well, so let's review the key questions, featured leaders, and the changes that faith-based leadership challenges us to make.

LEADERSHIP REBORN

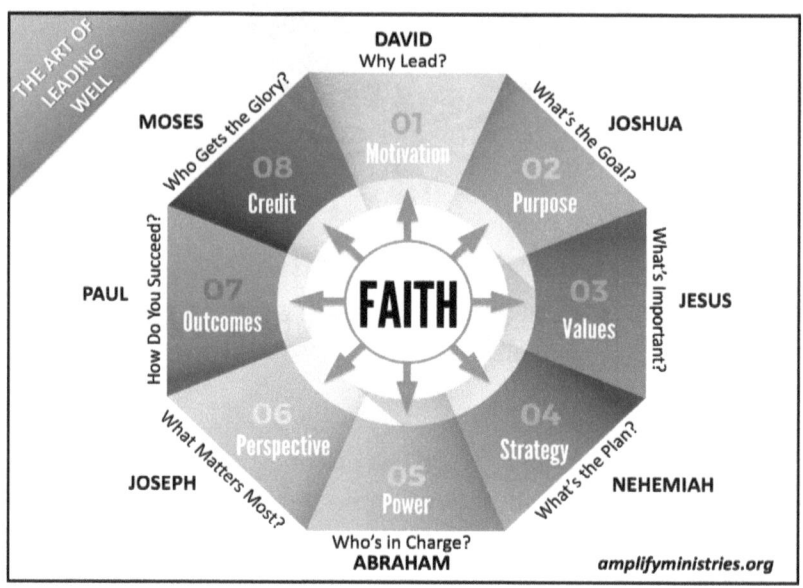

Again, the diagram above is a visual representation of what it looks like to have our faith infuse all aspects of our leadership. When our faith is at the center of our leadership, it fuels our motivation, purpose, values, and strategy, and it shapes our view of power, perspective, outcomes, and credit.

CHANGE IN MOTIVATION

From David's leadership and his heart for God, we learned how he was <u>called</u> to lead, how he was <u>committed</u> to God, that he was <u>challenged</u> to give up, how he was <u>confirmed</u> as king, and how he was <u>contrite</u> and open-hearted when he made mistakes. The key fundamental principle that David helped us address was a change in motivation: Why lead? Faith reframes our motivation, why we lead, and how we motivate others in three key ways. First, leading well starts with the leader's heart. Faith-based leadership begins with an open heart toward God and a willingness to follow His leading in our lives. Second, our faith becomes a powerful motivator in our leadership because it adds a spiritual aspect to why we lead. The reason we lead takes on a new meaning. Third, our faith can not only change our motivations for leading, but it can also change how we motivate others. Faith-based leadership finds ways to truly motivate and inspire people in honorable ways.

Key Question

How does infusing faith into your leadership affect your motivation?

CHANGE IN PURPOSE

From Joshua's leadership and the way he led the people of Israel, we learned about having a <u>cause</u> to believe in, his <u>courage</u> to lead, his <u>character</u> to honor God, his <u>conviction</u> to follow through, and the <u>covenant</u> he renews. The key fundamental principle that Joshua helped us address was a change in purpose: What's the goal? Faith refocuses our purpose and the goal of our leadership in three key ways. By establishing a healthy spiritual life, private life, and community life, our faith can reframe our leadership goals. Regarding our spiritual life, faith-based leadership requires that one of our primary goals is to honor God no matter what our leadership role is. Regarding our private life, leading with strong inner character and acting with personal and moral integrity is critical to the longevity and effectiveness of our leadership. Keeping a tight rein on our private lives is crucial to leading well. Regarding community life, faith-based leadership makes loving people a primary goal. If we are to lead well, we must care for the wellbeing of those under our leadership. In addition to other responsibilities, leading well means caring about the hearts, souls, and lives of others.

Key Question

How does infusing faith into your leadership affect your purpose?

CHANGE IN VALUES

From Jesus' leadership and the way he valued people, we learned about how He was <u>sent</u> by God, His <u>service</u> and <u>sacrifice</u> for others, and how He provides <u>salvation</u> and <u>support</u> for His followers. The key fundamental principle that Jesus helped us address was a change in values: What's important? Faith reprioritizes our values and what's important in three key ways. First, leading well requires biblical values at its core. The values of serving, humility, sacrifice, and love are elevated. Second, the value of people is paramount. Jesus valued people. He challenged people, loved people, and died for people. Faith-based leadership values people over profits, people over programs, and people over procedures. Third, leadership at its base level is rooted in relationships. Building healthy relationships with the people we lead, and team building, are vital to leading well because they build trust and connection.

Key Question

How does infusing faith into your leadership affect your values?

CHANGE IN STRATEGY

From Nehemiah's leadership and his strategy to rebuild Jerusalem, we learned how he prayed, planned, provided, protected, and prevailed. The key fundamental principle that Nehemiah helped us address was a change in strategy: What's the plan? Faith reforms our strategy and how we accomplish the plan in three key ways. First, a leader's strategy to accomplish goals and execute tasks must fit with the values and purposes of the Bible. Whatever plan a leader comes up with must be done in such a way that God is honored, people are valued, and morals are upheld because *how* we get there matters. Second, faith-based leadership invites God into the strategy development process. Pray over your strategies, business models, game plans, and goals. Ask God to help you and your team come up with effective, beneficial, profitable, and honorable ways to accomplish your objectives. Third, leading well means sharing the load. Lean on your team and delegate. Don't try to do it all yourself. Share the vision, mission, and goals. Then release them to get the job done using their unique gifts and talents.

Chapter 14

Key Question

How does infusing faith into your leadership affect how you develop strategies?

CHANGE IN POWER

From Abraham's leadership and the way he struggled for control, we learned that he was <u>faithful</u> to follow God, <u>fearful</u> of no heir, <u>forceful</u> of his own plan, <u>forgetful</u> of God's promises, and he found <u>freedom</u> in letting go. The key fundamental principle that Abraham helped us address was a change in power: Who's in charge? Faith releases control and changes our view and use of power in three key ways. First, faith-based leadership surrenders control up to God and leans on His wisdom and guidance. Leading well calls us to release control to God and trust His leadership over us. Second, faith-based leadership recognizes that our leadership is accountable to a higher power outside of ourselves or the organization. Ultimately, God is our boss. He is in charge, and we answer to Him regardless of our role or position. Third, leading well invites us to handle power wisely. Leading well requires us to share our authority and power with others. By putting the power in the hands of the people who must execute the plan, we empower them to lead alongside us.

Key Question

How does infusing faith into your leadership affect how you view and handle power?

CHANGE IN PERSPECTIVE

From Joseph's leadership and his struggle to gain perspective, we learned about the <u>pit</u> of betrayal, his <u>path</u> to Egypt, the <u>prison</u> of the forgotten, his <u>promotion</u> by Pharaoh, and the <u>preservation</u> of the people. The key fundamental principle that Joseph helped us address was a change in perspective: What matters most? Faith renews our perspective and what's most important in three key ways. First, faith-based leadership seeks to hold on to what matters most, and what matters most is that we hold on to our faith, no matter what. Our faith is foundational to our leadership, and it is vital for gaining any true and lasting perspective. Second, Joseph's journey helps give us perspective about how we view hardship. Faith-based leaders trust that God is present and at work even in our darkest times, deepest pain, and hardest difficulties. Faith-based leaders allow their faith to shine through their difficulties and trust that God will use their hardship for good in the end. Third, the faith-based leader looks to see the big picture and tries to view things from God's perspective. Our faith can help us step back from our circumstances and allow for the possibility that God may have a plan beyond our understanding and a purpose beyond what we can see.

Key Question

How does infusing faith into your leadership affect your perspective?

CHANGE IN OUTCOMES

From Paul's leadership and the way he viewed success, we learned about his <u>persecution</u> of believers, how he <u>pivots</u> toward God, his <u>provision</u> to lean on God, his <u>perseverance</u> to press on in his faith, and his desire to <u>pass</u> things on by handing off the leadership torch to others. The key fundamental principle that Paul helped us address was a change in outcomes: How do you succeed? Faith redefines success and how we view outcomes in three key ways. First, faith-based leadership redefines what a successful leader looks like. A faith-based leader pivots his or her leadership toward God and allows Him to shape how we lead others. Faith-based leaders realign their leadership styles, strategies, and methods to fit with biblical values in order to be successful. Second, faith-based leadership redefines our faithfulness to God as the most important outcome over and above any other leadership metrics. Faith-based leadership reframes traditional measurements of success in light of our individual and collective faithfulness to God first. Third, successful faith-based leaders persevere and pass on their leadership and their faith. Leading well means leaving a legacy of leaders beside and behind us who know how to lead well.

Chapter 14

Key Question

How does infusing faith into your leadership affect how you view and handle success?

CHANGE IN CREDIT

From Moses' leadership and the mistakes he made along the way, we learned about his role as a <u>servant</u> of the Lord, his <u>status</u> as God's chosen mediator, his <u>shift</u> in thinking, how <u>sin</u> crept into his heart, and how he had to <u>suffer</u> the consequences. The key fundamental principle that Moses helped us address was a change in credit: Who gets the glory? Faith redistributes the credit and who gets the glory in three key ways. First, faith-based leadership gives God the glory in all things. Leading well is not about personal glory, individual advancement, or achievement. The wise leader takes the compliments, praise, and success and gives God the credit. Second, infusing faith into our leadership requires a humble heart. Leaders who embrace their own humility, swallow their pride, and lift others up are easy to appreciate and follow. Third, faith-based leadership shares the credit with others. Leading well is about helping others succeed, elevating those around you, putting them in the spotlight, and winning as a team.

Key Question

How does infusing faith into your leadership affect how credit is given?

THE ENEMY OF OUR FAITH

From the tactics and strategies of Satan's leadership, we learned about him <u>deceiving</u> the world, <u>distorting</u> the truth, <u>delivering</u> temptation, <u>developing</u> darkness, and his goal of <u>destroying</u> humanity. The key fundamental principle that a look at Satan helped us address was a change in opposition: Who's our enemy? Faith redefines the battlefield and helps us identify the real enemy in three key ways. First, we look internally. Are there any areas of our life and leadership where the enemy of our faith might be lurking? In what ways are we being tempted? In what ways is the enemy trying to destroy our leadership, your character, and your effectiveness? Second, we look outward. Are there external factors opposing our leadership? If so, what are they? Are there any areas of your company, team, church, school, or family where the enemy might be lurking? Are there deceptions, lies, temptations, darkness, or destructive forces within your organization, team, or family? Third, we become discerning. Not all opposition to our leadership is spiritual, but some of it is. Faith-based leadership learns to see the difference between traditional obstacles and spiritual opposition and takes action to address them.

Key Question

How does infusing faith into your leadership affect how you view and handle opposition?

THE ENEMY'S DOMAIN

From how Satan has shaped the worldly environment we live in, we learned how he has distorted our perspective through our worldly culture, society's worldly values, people's worldly focus, individual's worldly motives, and our collective worldly pace. Over time, we can be fooled into building our lives on the wrong foundation. As a result, we end up thinking the wrong things; we focus on the wrong things; we want the wrong things, and we chase the wrong things. The key fundamental principle that the enemy's domain helped us address was a change in the world: Where's our enemy? Faith redefines our leadership landscape as we seek to lead others in a fallen world in three key ways. First, we look internally. How does the toxic environment of our worldly culture affect our leadership? In what ways has the enemy influenced your foundation, thinking, priorities, motives, and pace? Second, we look outward. How is the current worldly culture affecting your company, team, church, school, family, and the people you lead? Why is the world so uncooperative and resistant to faith-based leadership? Third, we become counter-cultural. Faith-based leaders learn to counter the cultural norms of a

Chapter 14

wrong foundation, wrong thinking, wrong priorities, wrong intentions, and the wrong speed with faith-based alternatives.

Key Question

How does infusing faith into your leadership affect your view of the environment and the culture in which you lead?

THE ENEMY WITHIN

From Adam's leadership and how his corrupt nature was passed along to us, we learned about the harsh reality of his <u>choices and consequences</u> and our <u>corrupt nature</u>, <u>corrupt hearts</u>, <u>corrupt minds</u>, and <u>corrupt behaviors</u>. The key fundamental principle that Adam helped us address was a change in nature: Why am I corrupt? Faith reveals a hidden enemy within us and highlights the inner battle that we all must face. To lead well, we must battle the enemy within ourselves and learn how to deal with the enemy within other people. Regarding the enemy within us, it's a leadership fact, leaders are flawed. Even the best leaders have flaws, shortcomings, and weaknesses. So how do we lead ourselves well considering this truth? It starts with admitting that we are not perfect, acknowledging our own corrupt nature, knowing our weak spots, and asking God to help. Regarding the enemy within others, it's a leadership fact, people are flawed. We lead in a world full of flawed, corrupted, and fallen people. So how do we lead fallen people? It starts with compassion and understanding. Remember the people and teams you lead are only human, so try not to let corrupt behavior surprise you. Sinful people sin. Offer correction; give guidance; and forgive often.

Key Question

How does infusing faith into your leadership affect how you view the nature of people?

VICTORY OVER THE ENEMY

From choosing to live a life of faith and developing our own leadership, we learned about how we can have victory over the enemy of our faith and the enemy within us. Victory comes as we <u>surrender to God</u> as we <u>start trusting,</u> <u>stop sinning</u>, learn to <u>stand firm</u>, and as we <u>seek accountability</u> from trusted friends. The key fundamental principle that a life of faith helped us address was a change in me: How can I win? Faith redefines our ability to overcome and gives us a new set of tools to achieve personal victory. By surrendering to God, trusting Him, resisting sin, standing firm in our faith, and seeking accountability, we can have victory over the unique enemies of faith-based leadership. While the struggle to lead well is ongoing, many faith-based leaders have found true and lasting victory over the enemy of our faith and the enemy within. It is possible to live a life of victory and lead victoriously. It takes a continual surrender to God, a disciplined mind and body, an understanding of God's Word, a reliance on Christ's strength in us, and a fair amount of leaning on good friends. Through our faith, we can address the problem of corruption within our own hearts, tackle it with the power of God, and find victory over the darkness.

Key Question

How does infusing faith into your leadership affect how you pursue victory in your personal life?

SUMMARY

When our faith infuses our leadership, eight major fundamentals change:

1. **Motivation:** Faith reframes our motivation and why we lead.
   - David's Heart: *Psalm 51:10*

2. **Purpose:** Faith refocuses our purpose & the goal of our leadership.
   - Joshua's Goal: *Joshua 6:20*

3. **Values:** Faith reprioritizes our values and what's important.
   - Jesus' Example: *John 13:14-15*

4. **Strategy:** Faith reforms our strategy and the plans we make.
   - Nehemiah's Project: *Nehemiah 4:16-17*

5. **Power:** Faith releases control and recognizes who's in charge.
   - Abraham's Struggle: *Genesis 15:3-5*

6. **Perspective:** Faith renews our perspective and what's important.
   - Joseph's Journey: *Genesis 50:20*

7. **Outcomes:** Faith redefines success and how we view outcomes.
   - Paul's Secret: *Philippians 4:12-13*

8. **Credit:** Faith redistributes the credit and who gets the glory.
   - Moses' Mistake: *Numbers 20:12*

WRAP UP

Leading well is a journey. Sometimes we'll get it right and sometimes we'll make mistakes. Keep trying to improve, develop, grow, and become a better leader than you were before. There will be lots of ups and downs along the way and each leadership role has its unique challenges, high points, and low points. No one leads perfectly, but you can lead well.

While you may not agree with everything we have talked about, we hope that you have grown in your understanding and ability to lead well. Hold on to these principles, process them, and discuss them with your teammates, co-workers, and friends. Find ways to apply them in your leadership context and pass them along.

Thanks for joining us and for taking the time to develop your leadership and your faith. The art of leading well is a lifelong journey so keep leading, keep serving, and keep loving those around you. May God bless your leadership as you put His Word and these principles into practice.

Chapter 14

PUTTING IT INTO PRACTICE

As we conclude the book, reflect on what you have learned. Think about, discuss, and apply the following questions one more time.

Leadership Thoughts

1. Which featured leader can you relate to the most? Why?
2. Which chapter stood out to you the most? Why?
3. How has this book encouraged you in your leadership and faith journey?
4. How has this book challenged you to grow in your leadership and faith?
5. What are two to three leadership principles from the book that you hope to implement?
6. How will your faith and the principles you have read about change the way you lead?
7. Who are some people you know who would benefit from reading this book?
8. How can you share what you have learned with other leaders and teammates?

ABOUT THE AUTHORS

Pastor Larry Ely and Dr. Daniel Ely have 70 years of combined experience in leadership and ministry.

Pastor Larry Ely has over thirty years of experience in leadership and ministry as a student pastor, speaker, teacher, supervisor, writer, consultant, and coach. He currently works as the Director of Coaching at LEAD222 where he trains and mentors student ministry leaders. He is passionate about the need for better leaders and better leadership. Larry is a graduate of Taylor University where he studied Christian Education and Youth Ministry.

In addition, he has a Master's degree in Student Ministry from Indiana Wesleyan University. He is the founder of amplifyministries.org and serves as a local Network Coordinator for the National Network of Youth Ministries. He enjoys helping students grow in their faith, eating tacos at the beach, and going on adventures with his family. Larry and his wife have two wonderful sons in high school and college.

Dr. Daniel Ely is a retired Professor of Biology and Physiology, National Institute of Health (NIH) funded biomedical researcher, American Heart Association researcher, and NIH reviewer. During his tenure at the University of Akron, Dan was awarded Researcher of the Year, Teacher of the Year, and Professor Emeritus. He has over forty years of experience in leadership, teaching, research, and ministry.

During his career, he served in many leadership roles and has been the chairman of numerous university and state scientific positions. Dan holds a PhD in Medical Physiology from the University of Southern California. He has spent many years leading and mentoring young couples and students. Dan and his wife live in northern Florida and enjoy nature and living on the water.

ADDITIONAL PRODUCTS:
Leadership Reborn Resources

VIDEO COURSE
This high-quality Master Class is designed for the everyday leader on the go.

- 14 Sessions covering each chapter of the main book
- Engaging stories and principles hosted by Larry & his sons
- Each session is only about 15 minutes
- Watch at your own pace
- Login with your mobile device or laptop
- Follow along with the Study Guide
- Great for individual and team leadership development
- Site licenses are available for group or team viewing

To order products, visit us online at:
www.leadershipbooks.com/products/leadership-reborn-video-course
or at www.amplifyministries.org/leadership-reborn/

LEADERSHIP REBORN

STUDY GUIDE

Our in-depth Study Guide is a companion to the Video Course and includes:
- All 14 Leadership Sessions
- **THE STORY**: This sets up the theme and topic
- **THE WORD:** Featured Bible text for the topic
- **THE POINT:** The main focus
- **THE CHANGE:** How faith changes your leadership
- **THE SPOTLIGHT:** A highlight of leadership in action
- **THE APPLICATION:** Questions to help you put it into practice
- Order additional study guides based on your audience or team size
- Great for team training or individual study and pairs well with the main book

To order products, visit us online at: www.leadershipbooks.com
or at www.amplifyministries.org/leadership-reborn/

READING PLAN AND E-BOOK

- **READING PLAN**: 5-Day Bible Reading Plan based on the book to help leaders grow in their faith. This Leadership Devotional will be available in the Bible App.

- **E-BOOK**: A digital version of the main book will be available on most major reading platforms.

- To access available products, search Leadership Reborn in the related Apps or visit us online for more details.

    www.amplifyministries.org/leadership-reborn/

TEACHING SERIES

Would you like to teach this leadership content to your team, church, or company? Great! Here's a complete packaged resource to teach the book yourself.

- **TEACHING PACKAGE:** A 12-week message series will be available for leaders to teach the main book themselves. *(Series will include: message notes, outlines, teaching slides, discussion questions, and graphics- all as a digital download).*

To order products, visit us online at:

www.leadershipbooks.com

www.amplifyministries.org/leadership-reborn

SPEAKING

Invite the author to speak at your next Leadership Training event. Larry Ely is available to book for speaking engagements and team training for churches, companies, schools, universities, retreats, youth groups, workshops, seminars, and conferences.

For booking, visit us online at:

www.leadershipbooks.com/pages/larry-and-dan-ely-speakers-bureau

www.amplifyministries.org/leadership-reborn

STAY CONNECTED

Keep up to date with the authors.
- **WEB**: www.amplifyministries.org
- **YOUTUBE**: www.youtube.com/@amplifystudentministries
- **INSTAGRAM**: @amplify_ministries
- **FACEBOOK**: www.facebook.com
  (Search "Leadership Reborn" for our Group Page)

LEADERSHIP CHALLENGE

You are invited to join the **"5 Day Leadership Challenge."** Take 5 MINUTES for 5 DAYS to improve and sharpen your leadership. It's EASY to participate. Simply: Read, Comment, and Share.

- **READ** the daily article
- **COMMENT** on a key aspect
- **SHARE** it with a friend or teammate

CHECK IT OUT:
www.amplifyministries.org/leadership-challenge/

INDEX OF STORIES

1. WHY FAITH-BASED LEADERSHIP?
Story: The Solar System (p.7)

2. CHANGE IN MOTIVATION
Story: Coach Vince Lombardi (p.19)
Spotlight: John F. Kennedy and PT-109 (p.32)

3. CHANGE IN PURPOSE
Story: Apollo 13 Space Mission (p.37)
Spotlight: The Effects of COVID-19 (p.48)

4. CHANGE IN VALUES
Story: Reality TV Show "Undercover Boss" (p.53)
Spotlight: Core Values at Chick-fil-A (p.64)

5. CHANGE IN STRATEGY
Story: Women's Soccer Championship (p.67)
Spotlight: Volvo's Change in Strategy (p.78)

6. CHANGE IN POWER
Story: Alexander the Great (p.83)
Spotlight: Company Conflicts (p.93)

7. CHANGE IN PERSPECTIVE
Story: Microscopes and Telescopes (p.99)
Spotlight: Abraham Lincoln and Slavery (p.111)

8. CHANGE IN OUTCOMES
Story: Olympic Snowboarder Shaun White (p.115)
Spotlight: The Wright Brothers' Invention (p.127)

9. CHANGE IN CREDIT
Story: The Watergate Scandal (p.133)
Spotlight: The Rise and Fall of VeggieTales (p.143)

10.   THE ENEMY OF OUR FAITH
Story: Movie Plot Twists (p.153)
Spotlight: An Inside Look (p.162)

11.   THE ENEMY'S DOMAIN
Story: The Leaning Tower of Pisa (p.166)
Story: The Impact of Stress (p.175)

12.   THE ENEMY WITHIN
Spotlight: The Reality of Leading (p.190)

ACKNOWLEDGMENTS

First, we would like to thank God for helping make this book possible. We are grateful to the Lord for His leadership in our lives and for the amazing example of servant leadership that Jesus gives us.

Second, we would like to thank our families. We deeply appreciate the love that our families have shown us during this project. Thank you to Tina and Linda for supporting, praying, and encouraging us in our writing. A big thanks to Devon and Dray for their fantastic work with recording the Video Course. I, Larry, would personally like to thank my dad and co-author for all of his wisdom, ideas, stories, strength, prayers, and encouragement to write and complete this book. It was an honor to write together and share the leadership journey with him.

Third, we would like to thank our friends. A big thank you to all the people that contributed meaningful, inspiring, and thoughtful leadership quotes for the "In the Trenches" section of the book *(Brent, Matthew, Jacob, Devon, Tim S, Ani, Dray, Nick, Steve, Tim E, Tina, and Julie)*. Thank you for your faithful leadership and for living out so many of the principles of leading well.

Fourth, we would like to thank the Palm Coast Student Bible Study for listening, engaging, applying, and offering ideas as they were taught the entire leadership book on Thursday nights. Thanks for being a great test audience! A huge thanks to the core students of the group. We deeply appreciate their student leadership and faithfulness to grow in their faith during difficult times.

Fifth, we would like to thank the following groups and people: Hope*writers *(writing group)* for their support, encouragement, and writing resources; Ella Herlihy for her ideas and leadership of our writer's discussion group; Sarah Geringer for her editing and book launch expertise; Mindy Baker and Erin Marshall for their book proposal advice and guidance; Florida Christian Writers Conference for helping us make publishing connections; our publishing team at Leadership Books for helping make this book a reality.

Last, we would like to thank you the reader for investing in your own leadership development and supporting our project. We pray that God would use this book to help transform the way you lead.

Keep leading, keep serving, and keep loving those around you.

NOTES

[1] "Leadership Styles," *Corporate Finance Institute,* 2022, accessed March 25, 2023, https://corporatefinanceinstitute.com/resources/management/leadership-styles/.

[2] "4 Leadership Styles in Business: Leadership Style Quiz," *The University of Arizona,* 2022, accessed March 25, 2023, https://www.uagc.edu/blog/4-leadership-styles-in-business.

[3] Nicole P. Vogt, "ASTR 110G Introduction to Astronomy: Geocentric and Heliocentric Models," *New Mexico State University,* 2006, accessed August 22, 2023, http://astronomy.nmsu.edu/nicole/teaching/ASTR110/lectures/quickview.html.

[4] "National Football League," "Super Bowl," "NFL," *Green Bay Packers,* and *Pittsburgh Steelers* are all trademarks of the National Football League and/or National Football League Properties, 2024.

[5] "Reggie White," *Pro Football Hall of Fame,* accessed November 8, 2022, https://www.profootballhof.com/players/reggie-white/.

[6] Vince Lombardi Jr, *What It Takes to Be #1: Vince Lombardi on Leadership* (New York, NY: McGraw-Hill, 2001), 214-215.

[7] Ibid., 132.

[8] "John F. Kennedy and PT-109," *John F. Kennedy Presidential Library and Museum,* accessed March 1, 2023, https://www.jfklibrary.org/learn/about-jfk/jfk-in-history/john-f-kennedy-and-pt-109.

[9] William Doyle, *PT 109: An American Epic of War, Survival, and the Destiny of John F. Kennedy* (New York, NY: Harper Collins Publishers, 2015).

[10] Devon Ely (Senior Intern at Pursuit Aerospace, GA), interview and personal communication by Larry Ely, March 17, 2023.

[11] Jim Lovell and Jeffrey Kluger, *Lost Moon: The Perilous Voyage of Apollo 13,* (New York, NY: Houghton Mifflin Harcourt Publishing, 1994).

[12] Ron Howard (Director), 1995. *Apollo 13* [Film]. Universal Pictures.

¹³ Sean Covey, *The 7 Habits of Highly Effective Teens* (New York, NY: Fireside- Simon & Schuster, Franklin Covey Company, 1998), 26-27.

¹⁴ Ibid., 6.

¹⁵ Eugene Peterson, *A Long Obedience in the Same Direction: Discipleship in an Instant Society* (Downers Grove, IL: InterVarsity Press, 2000), 92-98.

¹⁶ Tim Elmore, *Habitudes- Images That Form Leadership Habits and Attitudes: The Art of Self-Leadership* (Atlanta, GA: Growing Leaders, Inc., 2004), 1.

¹⁷ Taylor University, "Taylor: A Magazine for Taylor University Alumni, Parents and Friends (Summer 2021)" (2021). Article "Breakthrough." *The Taylor Magazine (1963-Present).* 195. (p.31-21), accessed October 11, 2022, https://pillars.taylor.edu/tu_magazines/195.

¹⁸ Brent Glover (Worship Pastor at Salty Church, Flagler Beach, FL), interview and personal communication by Larry Ely, January 2, 2023.

¹⁹ John Maxwell, *The 21 Irrefutable Laws of Leadership: 10th Anniversary Edition* (Nashville, TN: Thomas Nelson, 2007), 222.

²⁰ Louie Giglio, "General Session #1," *National Network of Youth Ministries: Network Forum* (Denver, CO: NNYM, January, 2002.

²¹ Curt Fowler, "Core 4 Leadership at Chick-fil-A," *Values Driven Results with Curt Fowler,* 2016, accessed September 5, 2022, https://valuesdrivenresults.com/newsletter/core-4-leadership-chick-fil-exercise-joints-amazing-story-forgiveness/.

²² Chick-fil-A 405 at Jefferson (Los Angeles, CA), "Team Member Opportunity Guide: Core Four," *CFA405jefferson,* accessed April 26, 2023, https://www.cfa405jefferson.com/team-member-opportunity-guide.

²³ Tim Sanchez (CEO at Chick-fil-A, Palm Coast, FL), interview and personal communication by Larry Ely, March 16, 2023.

²⁴ Gavin Hood (Director), 2013. *Ender's Game* [Film], Based on the book by Orson Scott Card. Summit Entertainment.

²⁵ Åke Sandberg, "Enriching Production: Perspectives on Volvo's Uddevalla Plant as an Alternative to Lean Production," *Industrial and Labor Relations Review,* Vol. 50, February, 1995, downloaded December 2, 2022,

https://www.researchgate.net/publication/23543035_Enriching_Production_Perspectives_on_Volvo%27s_Uddevalla_Plant_as_an_Alternative_to_Lean_Production.

[26] Ibid., 108.

[27] Dray Ely (Squad Leader: Online Gaming), interview and personal communication by Larry Ely, January 23, 2023.

[28] James S. Hewett, *Illustrations Unlimited* (Wheaton, IL: Tyndale House Publishers, Inc, 1988), 102-103.

[29] "Infamous Company Power Struggles," *Pack and Send*, 2015, accessed March 22, 2023, https://www.packsend.co.uk/infamous-company-power-struggles/.

[30] Alex Sherman, "Extremely Awkward: Bob Chapek and Bob Iger Had a Falling Out... Rift Looms Over Disney's Future," *CNBC*, March 2022, accessed March 22, 2023, https://www.cnbc.com/2022/03/20/disney-ceo-chapek-iger-falling-out.html.

[31] Mike Calia and Alex Sherman, "Bob Iger Returns as Disney CEO, Replacing Bob Chapek After a Brief, Tumultuous Tenure," *CNBC*, November 2022, accessed March 22, 2023, https://www.cnbc.com/2022/11/21/bob-iger-named-disney-ceo-effective-immediately.html.

[32] Justin Ferrabee, "How It Feels To Lead: Planting Your Flag In The Milieu of Discomfort," *Forbes Finance Council*, February 2019, accessed August 2, 2021, https://www.forbes.com/sites/forbesfinancecouncil/2019/02/14/how-it-feels-to-lead-planting-your-flag-in-the-milieu-of-discomfort/.

[33] Nick Gutierrez (Multi-Unit Area Manager at Moe's Southwest Grill, Palm Coast, FL), interview and personal communication by Larry Ely, November 14, 2022.

[34] Barry R. Masters, "History of the Optical Microscope in Cell Biology and Medicine," *Encyclopedia of Life Sciences: ELS* (Chichester, UK: John Wiley and Sons, Ltd., September, 2008, downloaded December 1, 2022), 1-2.

[35] Henry C. King, *The History of the Telescope* (Mineola, NY: Dover Publications, Inc. 2003,1979,1955), 30-38.

36 Diane Tedeschi, "The Planet Detective," *Air and Space Quarterly*, (Washington, DC: Smithsonian National Air and Space Museum, Fall 2022), 25-39.

37 Susan Bell, "A Cosmic Conversation," *USC Dornsife Magazine: The Cosmos Issue* (Los Angeles, CA: University of Southern California, Fall 2021-Winter 2022), 17-20.

38 Harry V. Jaffa, *A New Birth of Freedom: Abraham Lincoln and the Coming of the Civil War* (Lanham, MD: Rowman and Littlefield Publishers, Inc., 2004), 259.

39 Abraham Lincoln, Don E. Fehrenbacher (Annotator), *Selected Speeches and Writings: Abraham Lincoln* (New York, NY: First Vintage Books, Library of America, 1992).

40 Roy P. Basler (Editor), "Abraham Lincoln on Perseverance," *Abraham Lincoln Online*, 2018, from *The Collected Works of Abraham Lincoln*, accessed April 14, 2023, https://www.abrahamlincolnonline.org/lincoln/speeches/persevere.htm.

41 Don E. and Virginia E. Fehrenbacher (Editors), *Recollected Words of Abraham Lincoln* (Redwood City, CA: Stanford University Press, 1996), 330-331.

42 Justin Ewers, "Abraham Lincoln's Great Awakening: From Moderate to Abolitionist." *U.S. News and World Report*, February 9, 2009.

43 Doris K. Goodwin, *Leadership in Turbulent Times*, (New York, NY: Simon and Schuster, 2018).

44 Michael Burlingame, *Abraham Lincoln: A Life*, (Baltimore, MD: Johns Hopkins University Press, 2008).

45 Tina Ely (Preschool Teacher), interview and personal communication by Larry Ely, February 6, 2023.

46 Team Tony, "The Determination of Shaun White: Unlocking Greatness in the Face of Failures and Obstacles," *Tony Robbins Podcast: Shaun White's Ultimate Redemption*, January 10, 2019, accessed March 6, 2023, https://wwwtonyrobins.com/podcasts/shaun-whites-ultimate/redemption/.

47 "Shaun White: Olympic Gold Medalist and Entrepreneur," *Leading Authorities, Inc.*, accessed March 6, 2023, https://www.leadingauthorities.com/speakers/shaun-white.

[48] John Branch, "Sometimes Shaun White's Troubles Start When He's 20 Feet in the Air," *The New York Times,* February 8, 2022, accessed March 6, 2023, https://www.nytimes.com/2022/02/08/sports/olympics/shaun-white-olympics-snowboard.html.

[49] Quentin Reynolds, *The Wright Brothers: Pioneers of American Aviation* (New York, NY: Landmark Books, Random House Pub.), 1950.

[50] G.D. Padfield and B. Lawrence, "The Birth of Flight: An Engineering Analysis of the Wright Brothers 1902 Glider," *The Aeronautical Journal* (Liverpool, UK: The University of Liverpool, December, 2003), 697-718.

[51] Jacob Netherton (Campus Pastor at Salty Church, Flagler Beach, FL), interview and personal communication by Larry Ely, December 12, 2022.

[52] John W. Dean, *Blind Ambition: The White House Years* (New York, NY: Simon and Schuster, 1976), 150-151.

[53] John W. Dean, *Blind Ambition: The End of the Story* (Palm Springs, CA: Polimedia Publishing, 2009).

[54] Phil Vischer, "General Session #1: Phil Vischer," *National Youth Workers Convention* (Cincinnati, OH: Youth Specialties, 2006.

[55] Matthew Ranck (Student Pastor at Crescent Beach Baptist, Crescent Beach, FL), interview and personal communication by Larry Ely, January 4, 2023.

[56] "The Best Betrayals in Movies: #4 Joseph D. Pistone in Donnie Brasco," *Fandango,* accessed January 11, 2022, https://www.fandango.com/movie-photos/the-best-betrayals-in-movies-355.

[57] Lauren Favre, "Study: Big City Crime More Likely in the Day," *US News and World Report,* 2019, accessed January 26, 2023, https://www.usnews.com/news/cities/articles/2019-06-12/study-finds-crime-in-big-cities-is-more-likely-during-the-day.

[58] Billy Gierhart (Director), 2016. *Agents of S.H.I.E.L.D.: Absolution* [TV Series], Season 3, Episode 21, created by Marvel.

[59] Tim Ehrhart (International Missions Strategist: HS Ministry at CRU, Orlando, FL), interview and personal communication by Larry Ely, May 24, 2023.

[60] Sarah Pruitt, "Why Does the Leaning Tower of Pisa Lean?" *History: A&E Television Networks, LLC.*, 2015, accessed January 31, 2023, https://www.history.com/news/why-does-the-leaning-tower-of-pisa-lean.

[61] Tom Brady, "Tom Brady on winning: There's 'got to be more than this,'" *Interview with 60 Minutes*, 2005, accessed February 6, 2023, https://www.youtube.com/watch?v=-TA4_fVkv3c.

[62] Steve Francis (Owner at Wellspring Builders: Commercial Construction, Nashville, TN), interview and personal communication by Larry Ely, March 16, 2023.

[63] Allan Eastman (Director), 2002. *Andromeda: The Prince* [TV Series], Season 2, Episode 10, created by Gene Roddenbury.

[64] Anni Orefice (Hotel and Restaurant Specialist, Germany), interview and personal communication by Larry Ely, March 1, 2023.

[65] Robert Greene, *The Laws of Human Nature, Chapter 9 Confront Your Darkside* (New York, NY: Viking, Penguin Random House LLC, 2018), 231.

[66] Julie Francis (Nurse Practitioner), interview and personal communication by Larry Ely, May 31, 2023.

www.ingramcontent.com/pod-product-compliance
Lightning Source LLC
Chambersburg PA
CBHW030242010526
44107CB00030B/1311/J